SOUL CARE

when the nest is empty

Edie Melson

SOUL CARE
When the Nest is Empty

Edie Melson

Bold Vision Books
PO BOX 2011
Friendswood, TX 77549

Copyright © Edie Melson 2024

ISBN 978-196-270509-7
Library of Congress Control Number 2024931874

All rights reserved.
Published by
Bold Vision Books, PO Box 2011, Friendswood, Texas 77549
www.boldvisionbooks.com

Published in cooperation with Blythe Daniel
Edited by Larry J. Leech II
Cover Art by © Tatyana Abramovich | Dreamstime.com
Cover Design by kae Creative Solutions
Interior design by WendyEL Creative

Published in the United States of America.

Unless otherwise noted, scripture quotations marked (ESV) are from The Holy Bible, English Standard Version® (ESV®), copyright © 2001 by Crossway, a publishing ministry of Good News Publishers. Used by permission. All rights reserved.

Scripture quotations marked (NLT) are taken from the Holy Bible, New Living Translation, copyright © 1996, 2004, 2007, 2013, 2015 by Tyndale House Foundation. Used by permission of Tyndale House Publishers, Inc., Carol Stream, Illinois 60188. All rights reserved.

Scripture quotations marked (NASB) are taken from the NEW AMERICAN STANDARD BIBLE®, Copyright © 1960, 1971, 1977, 1995 by The Lockman Foundation. Used by permission. All rights reserved. www.lockman.org

THE HOLY BIBLE, NEW INTERNATIONAL VERSION® NIV® Copyright © 1973, 1978, 1984 by International Bible Society® Used by permission. All rights reserved worldwide.

Scripture quotations marked (HCSB) are taken from the Holman Christian Standard Bible®, Used by Permission HCSB ©1999, 2000, 2002, 2003, 2009 Holman Bible Publishers. Holman Christian Standard Bible®, Holman CSB®, and HCSB® are federally registered trademarks of Holman Bible Publishers.

*This book is dedicated to
My Sister-friend, DiAnn Mills.
We've traveled many roads together—
through parenting, writing, and unexpected life events.
You are the one who gets me and knows
the worst parts of me while still
loving me.*

CONTENTS

Introduction 9

chapter 1 **RELEASING FEAR TO GOD** 13

    The Roots of Fear 15

    Fear of My Own Inadequacy 20

    Small Window, Wide View 31

    When Change Looks Scary 36

    Scripture Prescriptions 41

chapter 2 **EMBRACING POSSIBILITIES** 43

    Right or Left 45

    The Beauty of Letting Go 50

    Finding Joy When the Past Intrudes 55

    When a Parent is Truly Happy 60

    The God of Our Child's Decisions 65

    Scripture Prescriptions 71

chapter 3 **RELEASING SADNESS** 73

    When Not Hovering is Hard to Do 75

    Am I Focused on the Right Things? 80

    Running Toward Letting Go 86

    When the Empty Nest Looks Different 92

    Value in the New Normal 97

    Scripture Prescriptions 102

chapter 4 **FINDING JOY IN THE CHANGES** 103

    New Joy 105

    Super Bloom 110

    Letting Perfect Just Happen 115

    Rejoicing is *Not* Selfish 120

    White Space 125

    Scripture Prescriptions 130

chapter 5 **FOCUSING ON NEW MEMORIES** 131

    Sunset, Sunrise 133

    Encouragement When the Climb Has Been Hard . . . 139

    The Gift of Silent Stillness 145

    Experiencing True Joy in My Child's Independence . . 150

    Pushing *Them* into Joy 155

    Scripture Prescriptions 160

Acknowledgments 161

Meet Edie Melson 163

INTRODUCTION

Welcome to *Soul Care When the Nest is Empty*. I've personally gone through the empty nest experience three times and they've all radically different. The first was a thrown-in-the-deep-end-and-hope-I-can-learn-to-swim experience. Our oldest son decided to head straight to war after high school when he joined the military. That experience threw my husband and I, as well as our other sons into emotional chaos.

I figured since I'd had that experience, the next two empty nest situations would be a walk in the park. Yeah, not so much. When our middle son left for college he was broke and wouldn't accept help from us. So, he spent his first two semesters living in his truck in a parking lot near campus. Talk about feeling like a parental failure.

When our youngest got ready to leave for college—following the expected path—I was ready. Or so I thought. When he left home, I spiraled into an unexpected—by me—depression. I cried off and on for six months straight.

All this to say, I get it. I know, through personal experience, that the circumstances of the empty nest can vary widely from person to person and even child to child in the same home. The most important thing I learned is that our crazy emotions—good and bad, happy and sad, and everything in between—aren't wrong. It doesn't make me a bad parent to cry, nor does it make me a bad parent to celebrate.

Not turning to God for help is the only thing that makes the empty nest season more difficult than it needs to be. He may not always provide the answer to *why*, but He always walks through the valleys with us. More importantly, He walks with our kids through this uncertain season. He's there when we can't be, and He orchestrates everything our kids need—when they need it.

I hope you enjoy the walk through this book, and I pray God will use it to draw you closer to Him.

Blessings,

Edie

Optional Supply List

My desire is for this book to be something you use. My prayer is that it will become dog-eared and stained from carrying it around. I urge you to draw in it, experiment, and again learn the healing power of play—especially play with our Heavenly Father.

You can use this book with nothing more than a pen or pencil. But if you want to go further, here is a list of supplies you might enjoy using:

- Colored pencils
- Markers, fine tip, brush, and/or glitter
- Paint, acrylic and/or watercolor
- Washi tape
- Stickers
- Gelato sticks
- Journal
- Glue
- Glitter
- Ribbon

In addition, I include several instances where I encourage you to take a photograph. You don't need special equipment.

- Cell phone camera
- An Instamatic of some kind, like Fujifilm
- Instax or Polaroid Snap
- Digital camera

chapter one
RELEASING FEAR TO GOD

Fear.

All parents struggle with a myriad of fears when it comes to our kids. We worry about their safety, their success, and their peer group. We all put boundaries in place to help protect our kids.

For me, fear is fed by my lack of control. While my kids grew, that illusion of control I held so tightly to disappeared like sand in a clenched fist. When I accepted that the ultimate responsibility for my children's well-being didn't rest with me, a new wave of terror took hold.

This struggle was hard and something I'm not proud of. I had to begin living like I believed what I'd always professed—that God loved my kids more than me. That my Heavenly Father was worthy of my trust. I knew in my head I could trust Him, but living that out brought me to a crisis point.

The foundation of my anxiety when our kids flew the nest was two-fold—fear and control. I'm not proud to admit my shortcomings in this regard, but I believe I'm not alone in the challenge of learning to let God be God in my kids' lives.

My fear came from my over-active imagination of things that could go wrong when I wasn't close by. These fears were fed by the misguided belief that I could control things when I was nearby. Truthfully, neither of these perspectives is accurate. I know—when I stop to think about it—that I am *never* in control. And there is not a time when God is *never* out of control.

Even knowing these truths—through experience and through Bible study—it's been a process to finally let go, moving on to embrace this very different stage of life. I've been helped by those in my community who've gone before me, as well as those who've walked through it with me.

Knowing others have struggled and triumphed has helped me through this transition.

THE ROOTS OF FEAR

I sought the Lord, and he answered me and delivered me from all my fears. (Psalm 34:4 ESV)

I am not a gardener. I'm the opposite—a grim reaper of plants. I love greenery and flowers, but I can't seem to turn that love into the ability to keep from killing them. Knowing this flaw made things worse—I'd over-water them, drag them from room to room trying to find the best light, and always over-mother them to death. In truth, I was battling my own root issues.

One day I inherited several precious plants that were over fifty-years old. It was such an honor to be entrusted with these living legacies—and my worst nightmare. How was I going to keep them alive?

I shared my fear with a friend. She explained plants that old have a hardy root system. These older plants had been through a lot and could withstand the learning curve my care would entail. The one thing she warned me against was hovering over them. I'd have to curb my fear and have faith in the roots they'd developed.

Fast forward several years and my friend was right. The plants are thriving so I'm beginning to relax my vigilance. But the whole process was a lot like releasing my kiddos into the world as they left the nest.

I had to learn to rely on the way God had equipped them for this new stage of life—curbing my fears and having faith in the roots they'd developed. God and I had several long talks about allowing Him to prune the fear that had taken root. Letting God prune my fear was a process, but once I'd acknowledged what was happening, He helped me change, and I was able to let go of the fears.

A PRAYER
to Help Me Trust God

Have I not commanded you? Be strong and courageous! Do not be terrified nor dismayed, for the LORD your God is with you wherever you go. (Joshua 1:9 NASB)

Dear Lord, in my mind I know You love my child more than me. I also know You have a plan for his life. But I'm so scared and my mind can't overcome my fears. I know his struggles and I can see all the possible ways my son can be led astray.

Help me change my focus and control my worries. Remind me of the foundation you've already laid in my son's heart and mind. Replace every fearful thought with a memory of how You've already protected him and brought him through difficult times.

Show me again how You are going before him and preparing his way out into the world. I'm excited about the possibilities before him. Why can't I rejoice and let go of the fear? Instead of letting go, I let my worries overshadow the joy.

Take my fears—again. I lay them at Your feet, acknowledging You are God and I am not. Show me how to dwell in peace as my son begins a new chapter in his life. Amen

CREATIVE CONNECTION:
Five-fingered Prayer for Letting Go

Part of my struggle with letting my kids fly off into the world comes from control issues—and a lack of trust. I created this prayer outline to help me remember to trust God with my kids, just like I trust Him in other aspects of my life.

Supplies

- ❏ This book
- ❏ Separate, blank piece of paper
- ❏ Pen
- ❏ Scissors
- ❏ Colored pencils

Directions

1. On the blank paper, trace your hand with your fingers spread out.
2. Cut out your hand shape.
3. Write out each of the following prayer prompts on one of the four fingers and thumb:
   a. Pointer finger: Priority
   b. Middle finger: Discovery
   c. Ring finger: Remembrance
   d. Little finger: Peace
   e. Thumb: Foundation
4. While looking at your drawing, make a fist of your own hand. Beginning with your thumb, release

each digit and say a prayer with that focus. For example, with your thumb you might pray this:

> Lord, I know you've given my child a firm foundation. Help me and my son both stand firm in all you've shown us.

5. Continue releasing your fist one step—one prayer at a time.
6. Use the space below to rewrite your five-fingered prayer. Add your thoughts on what God has revealed.

FEAR OF MY OWN INADEQUACY

And we know that in all things God works for the good of those who love him, who have been called according to his purpose (Romans 8:28 NIV)

Fear is a funny thing. It can attack us in many ways. If we're not careful, this deception can keep us from staying focused on the true issues.

For me, fear can attack through my own insecurity as a parent. I must constantly battle my own feelings of how I've failed my child. I know the things I've done—and not done—that have hurt my child. But, no matter what, God is bigger than my mistakes. I didn't accept the truth of this until I looked back at my childhood. None of us have had perfect parents. All of them—just like us—made mistakes.

I was struggling with frustration one day, aggravated that my almost-grown child had again refused to listen to what I'd told him to do. He'd called us—for the second time that night—to ask his father and I to bring him an extra key to his car. Yep, he'd locked his keys in the car twice in one night.

We had gone over ways to keep this common occurrence from happening. We'd purchased extra keys for his wallet and magnetic key boxes, but nothing had worked. On the way up to the movie theater to give our son his key, our sense of the ridiculous exerted itself.

By the time we reached our son, we both were recovering from a fit of the giggles. He stood, forlorn, beside his car. Every part of his body language was braced for the angry reaction he expected from us. What he found instead were two sympathetic parents. Along with rediscovering our sense of the ridiculous, my husband and I had remembered all the stupid things we'd done as teenagers and how our parents had reacted. Those parental scoldings hadn't helped us do better, instead they'd reinforced the picture of inadequacy we both still battled.

On the way to rescue our son, we'd made a conscious decision to build him up, instead of tearing him down. Now, please hear my heart. I am not bashing our parents. They did the very best they could and we're both grateful to have been raised in the families where God put us. I've learned that sometimes the mistakes of those before us can be used by God to help us make wiser choices.

That legacy of learning from others continues into our children today. God can and will use our mistakes—as well as what we did right—to shape our children into the people He has planned.

I'll add one other thing.

God knew all the parenting mistakes I'd make with my sons—and He still chose to give them to me. God didn't shake His head in regret when I messed up and wonder how He could have forgotten I was going to do that. No! God has chosen to work through my inadequacies, as well as my strengths.

Our God is able—in the good times and in the bad ones—to use life's circumstances to take care of our children and help them grow into the men and women He has planned.

A PRAYER
When My Inadequacy Overwhelms Me

If we confess our sins, He is faithful and righteous to forgive us our sins and to cleanse us from all unrighteousness. (1 John 1:9 HCSB)

Dear Lord, I'm such a horrible failure as a parent. I've made so many mistakes and now I'm almost sick with the thought that those mistakes will harm my daughter. I know I've asked forgiveness for my shortcomings and sins, and I accept You've forgiven me. And yet, I'm so fearful of the possible consequences.

Help me understand how You can bring good from bad. I know You promise *not* to punish the children for the sins of their parents. I also know that there are tendencies handed down in families, and these things crop up again and again. Oh, Lord, please break the cycle of these generational sins.

My daughter is now living away from me. I can't hover and anticipate the struggles she'll face. My imagination overwhelms me when I remember all the mistakes I've made. Remind me of the ways You've been bigger than my mistakes. Bring to my mind all the ways You've anticipated and changed my own shortcomings to blessings.

I know I can trust You, even—especially—with my daughter. Don't let me lose sight of that truth and hold tightly to it when my emotions and fears threaten to overwhelm me. Amen.

CREATIVE CONNECTION:
The Key to Peace

What is our key to overcoming inadequacy? It's the same key that unlocks peace—God. He is the one who can calm our fears and restore peace when inadequacy overwhelms us. This exercise will help us remember all that God is and the ways He helps when we only reach out to him.

Supplies

- ❏ Bible
- ❏ A key (you can use a real metal key, or you can trace one on a sheet of paper or cardstock and cut it out)
- ❏ Paper (or premade cardstock labels with a hole in the top to attach ribbon or twine)
- ❏ Various short lengths of ribbon or twine
- ❏ Pen

Directions

1. Begin by looking up several verses about peace. You'll need at least three.
2. Depending on the size of the label, either write the verse or the reference on each label.
3. Affix the label to the key with ribbon or twine.
4. Hang the key where you can see it. Mine is on one of the hooks where we keep our keys. Every time I reach for my keys, I see this visual reminder that God is the key when parenting overwhelms me.

UNDER THE SHELTER OF *WHOSE* WINGS

How precious is Your mercy, God! And the sons of mankind take refuge in the shadow of Your wings. (Psalm 36:7 NASB)

Certain images come to my mind when I think of being a parent. One that had the longest impact was a picture of a mother bird, still on her nest after a forest fire. She had not survived, but the baby birds safe under her wings had lived. I first saw this image when my kids were in grade school and middle school. I wanted to be that kind of a mother—the kind who would do anything to keep her kids safe and protected.

In some ways, I adopted that image as a goal of how I'd approach parenthood from then on. I took on the job of protector as one of my primary tasks, and I took that role seriously. I agonized over every parenting decision. Should I allow this? Have this in the house? Encourage this friend group? Every aspect was weighed against what could happen. Truly it was an exhausting way to parent children.

And this method was not God's design for parents.

I'd done something I shouldn't. I'd stepped from my role as a parent into God's role. This place wasn't one that God had designed me for. Unfortunately, I'm not necessarily a fast learner. I kept up this charade for much longer than I should have. One of our kids was the reason I saw the mistake I'd made.

Our son wanted to go somewhere with his church group—for all the right reasons. I was worried because I wouldn't be along on the trip to supervise. He could see I was well on the way to saying no when his words stopped me in my tracks.

"Mom, I know you're worried about me doing this. But truthfully, if I'm in God's will, I'm going to be just as safe there as I would be here."

We stared at each other for a few moments before I nodded. He was exactly right, not that something couldn't happen when he was following God's path. but more importantly God would be there to take care of him no matter what. We let him go on the trip and it was a great experience with no mishaps.

When it came to say goodbye as each of our sons flew the nest, I still thought about that bird. In so many ways I wanted to keep them tucked safely under my wings. But the truth I'd finally accepted was that they were already safe under Someone else's wings.

And covered by God is where the only true protection can come.

A PRAYER
When I'm Afraid to Let Go

"Let not your hearts be troubled. Believe in God; believe also in me. (John 14:1 ESV)

Dear Lord, You know what a control freak I am, and how much I try to control everything and everyone around me. This tendency is getting me into trouble again. I'm struggling to let my daughter go as she leaves the nest.

I can't get that image of the bird in the forest after the fire out of my mind. And I keep thinking, what would have happened to those precious babies if she hadn't been there? Lord, I want to be there, protecting my kids from every fire they encounter. Yet I know this is not Your design.

Your plan is a much better one. Each of us is to rely on You to be our covering no matter what comes. I love that for me, so why do I have so much trouble accepting this plan for my children?

Help me let go and truly turn them over to You. I know You already have them in Your tender care. I've watched how You've protected them when I couldn't be there. You've even protected them from my own poor judgement and missteps.

Be merciful and remind me of Your faithfulness. I should be stronger in my faith. I ask You to forgive me for my fear. Hold my hand as I let go of my daughter's hand. You are trustworthy. You are faithful and I know Your plans for my child far exceed anything I could hope or imagine. Amen.

CREATIVE CONNECTION:
True North

Sometimes, when I find myself afraid to let go, the best thing I can do is get up and get outside. This exercise has helped me reorient myself. Periodically I've found I need to go over the responsibilities of God versus my responsibilities. God is the true north in my life.

Supplies

- ❏ Compass (don't panic, most smart phones have a compass)
- ❏ This book
- ❏ Pen

Directions

1. Begin by grabbing your compass, this book or a journal, your pen and take a walk. You can walk near your home or visit a park or a special place. Just make sure the location is a familiar one.
2. Before you begin, look in the direction of true north. Take a moment and ask God to use this time to renew your sense of God's true north.
3. While you walk, don't hold your compass or try to follow the compass points, just walk the path you'd normally use. After about a block, look again at your compass. Do this throughout your walk.

4. When you're done with your walk, answer these questions in this book or your journal:
   a. How far have you veered from true north?

   b. Are you surprised or do you have a good sense of direction? (I have a horrible sense of direction. I have trouble telling West from Up.)

   c. What about your walk with God?

   d. How far have you veered from God's true north?

   e. Are you surprised or do you have a good sense of spiritual direction?

   f. What do you think God is trying to show you through this exercise?

   g. Finish by praying and thanking God that He is always with us to provide the direction we need.

SMALL WINDOW, WIDE VIEW

Behold, I have engraved you on the palms of my hands; your walls are continually before me. (Isaiah 49:16 ESV)

I love to take photographs. One of my favorite pastimes is wandering around a scenic place with my husband and my camera. Beyond the joy of taking pictures in our beloved Blue Ridge Mountains, I've also been able to expand my horizons and travel to amazing places, most recently Israel.

While I was there, I was fascinated by the ruins we toured. Walking through these ancient places, peeking into crevices and through openings in the stonework, brought me incredible joy. Sometimes these glimpses also led me to unexpected views. These small windows opened into glorious vistas, providing perspectives on the past I'd never have noticed otherwise.

Life as a parent is just like that. God sometimes provides those glimpses into our children's lives. That happened to me one time. I was watching one of our sons pull out of the driveway in his car and I immediately flashed back to when he got his first radio-controlled car. We'd helped him learn the basics of how to use it, given him some safety instructions, and finally let him play with it in our driveway. I remember that I'd been wondering what it would be like when he learned to drive a real car and began praying for that time—even though it was still years away.

Thinking back on those half-forgotten prayers, I could see how God had and was continuing to answer them. It struck me that even when I forget the specifics I prayed on my children's behalf, God never does. And God is still at work answering those prayers with my kids' **best** interests in mind.

A PRAYER
for Perspective

Think about the things of heaven, not the things of earth. (Colossians 3:2 NLT)

Dear Lord, here we are at the threshold of yet another season of life. I'm struggling to let go this time. I'm going to miss my son so much and all I want to do is hold on to him and keep him safe at home.

Give me your perspective. Help me see something that will give me more confidence in letting go and strengthen my faith in You.

I know you love my son even more than I do. Keep reminding me of the tangible ways You've loved him in the past. Bring to my memory specific times when I've seen You work on his behalf. Then use that to help me let go.

Don't let me stay where I am, paralyzed by fear of the future. I want to look at what's ahead for my son and feel peace. I know that can only come from You. Grow my faith as You again teach me to be a good parent. Amen.

CREATIVE CONNECTION
A Trip Down Memory Lane

When we're faced with the reality of letting go, we sometimes shy away from memories because they're just too painful. I've found, even if the initial step down memory lane is difficult, going farther often brings peace and joy. That's the purpose of today's creative exercise.

Supplies

- This book or journal
- Old photo album or picture or an object from your child's earlier years
- Pen

Directions

1. Begin with prayer, asking God to give you a new perspective on the memories you're about to explore.
2. Choose a picture or object to focus on.
3. Close your eyes and reconstruct all that was happening around this picture or object. Think about all the following:
   a. the day
   b. the time of year
   c. the people nearby
   d. the state of the world when this picture was taken (or object was used)

    e. who was in your immediate and extended family
    f. any songs, television shows, movies, or books that come to mind
    g. how your child has grown since that place in time, physically, mentally, and spiritually
    h. how you have grown, physically, mentally, and spiritually
4. Now write what you've discovered and what God has shown you.
5. End with a prayer asking God to continue to reveal more memories.

WHEN CHANGE LOOKS SCARY

See, I am doing a new thing! Now it springs up; do you not perceive it? I am making a way in the wilderness and streams in the wasteland. (Isaiah 43:19 NIV)

We took the plunge and moved—downsizing in the process. It was a big change and I have to confess I'm not usually big on change. There have been a lot of challenges, but the blessings of our new situation have far outweighed the stress.

One of the unexpected joys has been our small garden spot where the hummingbirds come to play. I love hummingbirds and because of the way our old home was situated on the lot, we never could have a feeder close to the house. But here, the feeder and the flowers are right outside our cozy screened porch.

I've learned a lot about these active visitors and they're around so much that I can now identify them by the markings. They are incredibly active. To keep up their energy they must drink about one third of their body weight a day. Normally their wings beat around fifty to seventy-five times a *second*, but during mating or fights, that can increase to two hundred beats.

Thinking back on my time as an active parent, I've often felt like I used to move at that speed. But even in the midst of the busyness, I knew a new season loomed on the horizon. I'd been reassured by others who'd walked the path before me that my child would need me just as much after they left home, but living that out would look very different.

Have I mentioned I'm not a fan of change?

That shift in daily life was hard. It brought joy, of course. I celebrated each of our son's accomplishments and independence—even as I mourned the passing of time. I had to remind myself to look for the joy. Just like learning to identify each individual hummer in my backyard, joy became something I recognized.

The rhythm of life changes. That's part of God's plan—a good part—not a bad one. But that doesn't mean it's not hard. Some seasons are marked by almost insane busyness, and others with time to reflect. But being a parent never ends and that's a source of joy no matter what stage of life our kids are in.

A PRAYER
for the New Rhythm of Life

He who calls you is faithful, who also will do it. (1 Thessalonians 5:24 HCSB)

Dear Lord, I'm leaving a busy time of life and moving on. I should be glad about the change of pace, but I'm not a big fan of change. I want to embrace this next season fully, but as I look ahead, I see only all the things that might go wrong. The lack of busyness looks sad and like something I don't want to experience.

Please help me see the future from your perspective. I know your plans are best for all of us, but they still seem frightening. I'm fearful that I won't be as important to my daughter as I have been.

This new rhythm looks lonely. Show me my place from a different perspective. Help me remember all things I've been too busy for up until now. Help me refill my life with healthy hobbies and meaningful work.

I know that I'll never stop being a parent. Help me walk into my new role of empty nest parenting with grace and confidence, instead of the fear I'm feeling. I don't want to steal my daughter's excitement because I'm sad.

Thank you for walking through this with me and for already having a plan to bring about a victory in this struggle. Amen.

CREATIVE CONNECTION
Fear to Faith

It's easy to hold onto fear and difficult to embrace faith that helps us accept the difficult seasons in life. But moving from one to the other is a discipline we each must practice. Today's creative connection will help with that process. I love playing with words. Working with an acrostic is a great way to do this.

Supplies

- ❏ This book
- ❏ Pen
- ❏ Colored pencils
- ❏ Decoration for this page

Directions

1. Begin with prayer. Ask God to show you the process of moving from fear to faith. Notice that fear is a shorter word than faith. I chose these two words because fear isn't as powerful as faith *in God*. This is just another way to illustrate that truth.
2. Use the letters in the two words on the next page to make an acrostic, adding words and phrases describing what you need to move from fear to faith.

F

E

A

R

F

A

I

T

H

SCRIPTURE PRESCRIPTIONS

- *For God has not given us a spirit of fear and timidity, but of power, love, and self-discipline. (2 Timothy 1:7 NLT)*

- *Do not fear them, for the LORD your God is the One fighting for you. (Deuteronomy 3:22 NASB)*

- *Peace I leave with you; my peace I give to you. Not as the world gives do I give to you. Let not your hearts be troubled, neither let them be afraid. (John 14:27 ESV)*

chapter two
EMBRACING POSSIBILITIES

God designed us—and the world we live in—with purpose and meaning. In nature, there's a reason for every season. In our own lives, we were created for specific rhythms. Daily we have a time for activity and a time for rest. Weekly we see a time for busyness and time for the Sabbath. As parents we have years of constant care and oversight, followed by a time of letting go.

When we've spent so long in the season of daily care and concern, letting go of that familiar rhythm can bring unexpected stress. Our emotions may not immediately fall in line with what we think we should be feeling. If you—like me—battle a tendency to want to control circumstances, this lack of control brings more anxiety than anticipation.

God's plan is for us to release our worries about what can go wrong. Instead, we look toward what can go right—in our children's lives and in our own changed circumstances. We've seen God work in their lives, bringing good from difficult. He is the same yesterday, today, and tomorrow. We can rest in the fact that He will continue to bless our children—in spite of poor choices, bad companions, or anything else we fear.

Beyond bringing good from bad, we know God has amazing things planned for our kids in this new season. God has already been at work preparing them for the new things He's going to be doing. As their parents, we get a front row seat to watch God's plan unfold.

We can also anticipate the plans God has for us in this season. We've been about the business of daily parenting and now He has a new season for us. Some may have already received confirmation about what's to come. Others may feel adrift and almost forgotten, but God has *not* forgotten us. We are just as vital to His plans as we were the day we became parents.

It's time to embrace the possibilities of what God is about to do. He will bless us and our kids with exceeding abundance, often when we least expect it. Instead of being ambushed by the good, let's begin expecting God's coming gifts.

RIGHT OR LEFT

For I know the plans I have for you"—this is the LORD's declaration—"plans for your welfare, not for disaster, to give you a future and a hope. (Jeremiah 29:11 HCSB)

I remember when My husband and I visited a new restaurant. He drove, but I was the one who knew exactly where the restaurant was, although he was familiar with the general area. We came to one intersection and I told him to turn right. He disagreed and said he wanted to turn left. I told him you can turn left if you want, but the correct way is right. He grinned. "So I go right or I can go left." His emphasis on the word made it a choice between right and wrong instead of just directions.

The truth—which we both knew—was that turning either way would have gotten us where we wanted to go, but I was claiming my way was the only *right* way. We both giggled over his play on words and continued to dinner. But the phrase stuck in my mind.

One of my biggest worries about my kids leaving home was the decisions they'd make without wise input. I knew that often our life decisions can take us places we never wanted to go, or delay getting to our goals. When our sons were at home, I could keep a watchful eye on their decisions and often head off calamity. Or so I thought.

The truth is, God knows the best path to where He wants us to be. Even when we get off that path, He works things out so our mistakes add benefit and often blessings to the journey. I've done a lot of biting my tongue since our kids left home. But I've learned that their choices aren't etched in stone and there's rarely a single right and wrong answer when God's involved. He is the God of second chances, and third, and fourth.

And no matter if our kids chose right or left, we're never left far from God.

A PRAYER
for Letting My Child Choose Their Own Path

The father instantly cried out, "I do believe, but help me overcome my unbelief!" (Mark 9:24 NLT)

Dear Lord, help me stop trying to control my child's path. You have orchestrated this new season of independence for him. You are walking with him and this should be enough for me. Forgive me for my lack of faith.

I remember all the mistakes I made when I was young. And I have the experience of so many more years and circumstances. I can't seem to keep from offering direction. Put a lock on my tongue and keep me from giving unasked-for advice.

I know my child's path is *supposed* to be different from mine, but I want to save him heartache and difficulty. Even though my motives come from a parent's love, I admit I am not You. Your perspective is perfect, and so is Your plan for His life. I know my trust in You is overdue. So, once again, I'm consciously choosing to release him into Your care. You are trustworthy and I thank You for Your patience and love. Amen.

CREATIVE CONNECTION
Remembering My Child's Strengths

Sometimes we struggle when our kids take paths we wouldn't have chosen for them. We start believing the lie that they're destined to disaster. When we do that, we've forgotten that God has already equipped them for what they're facing. Beyond that, the struggles they—and we—face are specifically chosen to make us more Christ-like.

Today's creative connection is a journaling exercise to help us remember the wonderful gifts God has given our children.

Supplies

- ❑ This book
- ❑ Pen
- ❑ Things to decorate the page (colored pencils, stickers, washi tape, etc.)

Directions

1. Pray first, asking God to bring to mind the many strengths He's gifted your child with.
2. Begin making a list of each strength your child has. After each one, include a sentence or two about how you've seen him use that strength.
3. End with a written prayer, thanking God for the path your child is on right now.

THE BEAUTY OF LETTING GO

On the glorious splendor of Your majesty And on Your wonderful works, I will meditate. (Psalm 145:5 NASB)

Autumn is my favorite time of year. I love the unexpected colors, the crispness of the weather, and I love the sky. To me, there isn't a blue that compares to a clear blue sky in October. One day I finally researched the reason for that.

Without getting too deep into the science, lower humidity means there is much less of something called the Mie Scattering. Because of this, much more blue light reaches us and that makes the sky look bluer.

While I considered this, God brought to my mind some parallels to the process of becoming an empty nest parent. Just like in nature, my life as a parent began with spring—and with the addition of a new life to our home. That time of life overflowed with unexpected beauty and bounty. When the kids grew, we entered a season similar to summer. Every part of every day was busy—from carpools, to gatherings, to homework. And just like summer, I blinked and now that season is past.

With this autumn time of life, I find myself overwhelmed with changes. And saddened by what's to come. But again, God has provided inspiration when I look at this season in His perfect creation. In the changing leaves, I see unexpected colors and beauty beyond my ability to imagine. Those incredible colors wouldn't be possible unless the trees were getting ready to let go.

I find so much in this example in God's creation that I can apply to this time in my life. For one thing, when the weather changes gradually—when there's been plenty of rain—the fall colors tend to last longer, giving more time to experience the beauty. The changes are inevitable. Just like in nature, when I relax into the process as a parent, life is a much more beautiful place.

And I find it easier to embrace the process when my soul is well-watered through the presence of God in my life. When I stay in step with Him, through daily Bible reading and prayer time, I'm much more likely to feel God's comforting presence.

But there are times when I can't help but fight the process. And sometimes it takes a hard freeze to make me let go. In nature, when the weather turns abruptly, it can cause the trees to drop their leaves or make them turn an ugly brown. God does have a plan for me to let go of my children and allow them to fly the nest. This change will happen. My choice comes in how I weather the change—in step with God or protesting every inch.

A PRAYER
for the Process

You can make many plans, but the LORD's purpose will prevail. (Proverbs 19:21 NLT)

Dear Lord, I've spent my child's entire life holding on tight—to her and to You. I've worked hard to remain vigilant and keep her from all harm. And now my role is changing and I'm having trouble with the process of letting go.

I know that the time has come for my daughter to walk into her new life—without my constant supervision. I'm having so many doubts about how well prepared she is. Did I do all You asked me to do? Please keep her safe, in spite of my failings.

Give me peace about this time. Don't allow me to doubt You now, when I need You most. I know I can trust You to take care of my girl. You know what's ahead of her on life's journey and You are already there, preparing her path.

Don't let me forget all the ways you've gotten her ready for this new season. Don't let me hold on to her when I know it's time to let go. Instead, remind me to hold tight to You. You are our strength and our source of peace. Amen.

CREATIVE CONNECTION
Practicing the Art of Letting Go

Letting go takes practice. Today's creative connection will give us a chance to develop this skill.

Supplies

- ❏ This book
- ❏ Pen
- ❏ Bible
- ❏ Two smooth river rocks or two pieces of paper cut into the shape of a rock
- ❏ Paint pen

Directions

1. Begin with prayer. Ask God to use this exercise to show you something new about the process of letting go.
2. Consider one thing that is particularly difficult for you as your child leaves home. I found losing the daily interaction with him hardest.
3. Ask God to lead you to a specific Bible verse regarding this struggle.
4. On the first rock, write your struggle. In my case, I wrote two words—daily communication.
5. On the second rock, write either the Bible verse or the Bible verse reference.

6. Decorate each rock as much as you choose. Remember that some of us love the artistic process, others, not so much. The point of this is letting go, not creating a masterpiece.
7. Go outside and bury the rock that has your struggle written on it. Say a prayer as you do so, asking God to help you to discard your struggle, burying and forgetting this specific worry.
8. Put your rock with the Bible verse in a place you'll see it regularly. Use it to remind yourself *not* to dig up worries you've already given to God.

FINDING JOY WHEN THE PAST INTRUDES

You have made known to me the paths of life; you will fill me with joy in your presence. Acts 2:28 (NIV)

I stood in church one day when an old familiar song came into the singing rotation. The song was one we'd sung years ago, when the kids were little. I remember it because one of my most precious parenting memories is tied to that tune. I still remember that day like it was yesterday.

Our middle son was well beyond the toddler stage, but not quite at the point of being able to always keep still during service. I knew, even in the worship time, this was going to be an *active* day. To head off his fidgets, I did something I hadn't done in a while. Instead of fussing at him, I swung him up into my arms and held him close. We swayed in time to the music while I sung softly in his ear. His little body relaxed into mine and his arms reached up to give me a hug.

He was heavy, but I don't think there was anything that could have induced me to put him down and cut short that precious time. I knew, with a clarity that could only have come from God, that this would be one of the last times I'd have this experience with him and I wanted to savor every moment.

Fast forward many years and as that song played in church, my mind was flooded with the sensations of cuddling my now-grown son. While I wouldn't want to relive everything that life had brought us in the intervening years, part of me wanted the chance to return to that time. And I confess my eyes teared up with the knowledge I never could.

Life goes on—past the good stuff and the bad. Some days it's harder than others to let go of wishing and wanting. On those days I try to remember to give myself grace. I think remembering and regretting we'll never get to go back can be a healthy part of moving forward. Although I don't like to cry in public, I've learned the cathartic release my tears can bring. I've also learned that I can't dwell only in the memories. Now I look for ways that God might add to those memories with new precious moments. Moving forward, I can see a time when maybe that cuddle with my son will be echoed while I cuddle his children. Or, if that isn't part of my future, I can rest in the fact that God has beautiful memories yet to be formed.

A PRAYER
When the Past Intrudes

Do not remember the past events, pay no attention to things of old. (Isaiah 43:18 HCSB)

Dear Lord, it seems that the closer the empty nest comes, the more memories of my son as a child intrude. Everywhere I look, I'm reminded of those precious times. I don't want to ever lose those memories, but some days they're overwhelming. Tears seem to always be close to the surface.

Help me experience those flashbacks with joy. Use them to remind me that more precious memories are coming in the future. Help me look at what's to come with anticipation instead of dread. So many good things are happening in our son's life right now. He's so excited for the future. Let his enthusiasm about this new season infect me.

Give me the ability to stop looking at the memories as if nothing good will ever happen again. I know that's a lie. I know it's okay to be sad about the things that are ending. But don't let me choose to wallow in that sadness. Instead, replace what I'm losing with a glimpse of all that I'm gaining as my son grows. Show me how to pack the sadness away and unpack joy in this new season of life. Amen.

CREATIVE CONNECTION
Making a New Memory or Tradition

Sometimes the only way to relieve the regret of memories or traditions we can't repeat is to replace them with new ones. So, today's creative exercise is to plan a new memory with your child. I will give you some ideas, but the actual execution is up to you and your specific circumstances.

Supplies

- ❏ This book
- ❏ Pen
- ❏ Whatever else needed to carry out the memory-making endeavor

Ideas to form a new memory or tradition:
- ❏ Use your phone and begin a new text tradition by sending either a weekly or daily text of encouragement. Choose a day and time and repeat it regularly. Example: a Monday morning encouraging Bible verse or quote.
- ❏ Meet for a meal at a new place. Take a couple of selfies with your child and have one printed. Display the picture somewhere you'll see it regularly.
- ❏ When you and your child are together, plan an outing at a new place, it could be a picnic, a shopping expedition, or an outdoor adventure.

Directions

1. Begin with prayer and ask God to help you make a new memory with your child.
2. Make a plan, and write it here in this book.
3. Come back and report on how this exercise has helped.

WHEN A PARENT IS TRULY HAPPY

These things I have spoken to you, that my joy may be in you, and that your joy may be full. (John 15:11 ESV)

Years ago I read a quote that has stuck with me. Not because it's necessarily something I should take to heart, but because it troubled me. Depending on where you read the quote, it goes something like this: "A mother is only as happy as her least happy child." I've tried to find who originated these words with no luck. The words have been attributed to everyone from Jackie Kennedy to Tim Keller.

I'm not arguing with the possible truth that this happens. Many of us can get so caught up in the lives of our children that we let their circumstances dominate our lives. This quote bothers me because I truly don't believe the idea reflects *God's* truth. I pondered this quote and realized that if I'm not careful, I tend to live my life this way. That my happiness—or sadness—can ultimately only be dictated by someone else other than God is a sad commentary on my priorities.

I'm not talking about times when we are called to weep with those who weep. (See Romans 12:15.) The thing I've learned to guard against is letting my internal joy be dictated by someone else's circumstances, and to be honest, I've struggled a lot with this. When someone close to me, especially my child, is unhappy it's very hard for me to look beyond that.

I asked God to give me some insight on this. How do I walk the line between empathizing with my child and keeping the joy of the Lord my top priority in my life? I found that for me the answer has two parts. The first part comes with perspective.

When my kids were young, their hurts were mostly minor. I comforted skinned knees, hurt feelings, and their frustration at healthy boundaries. I knew these painful parts of childhood would be fleeting. These frustrations, and how we all dealt with them, would help prepare them for other circumstances. After processing this, I found I could better keep my perspective.

As they grew, the hurts they faced were harder—on me and on them. This is where the second part of the answer comes in—that of faith. Because I know God's character, I can have faith that He has a plan for my kids—even when they're hurting. With that faith comes peace, and the ability to accept joy in other parts of my life.

A PRAYER
for Joy

But seek first His kingdom and His righteousness, and all these things will be provided to you. (Matthew 6:33 NASB)

Dear Lord, I confess I've lost my priorities. Somehow I've begun to place my child's happiness over the joy You have for me. I know I'm believing the lie that feeling happy when my daughter is struggling is wrong. But it feels wrong to be happy when she's unhappy about this season.

I know not all kids are happy about moving into adulthood, but my child's struggle is overwhelming me. Show me the balance I need. I don't want her to feel like I don't care. In the space between indifference toward her feelings and constant pain at them is where I want to land.

Guide me into obedience. Show me how to handle this confusing time. I don't want my emotions to feed hers negatively. Instead, use me to help her return to joy and find the path you have for her.

Help me look up to You and see all the blessings in my life and once again experience joy. You have a plan for my life outside of parenting. Don't let me miss what You have for me because I'm so wrapped up in my child.

Give me peace about continuing on with my life even in the midst of her crisis. Only You know the right balance—that brings all of us joy. Don't ever let me put anyone or anything ahead of You in my heart. Amen.

CREATIVE CONNECTION
Planning a Joy Date

Sometimes being joyful takes some planning and deliberate choices. With this exercise, you'll plan and take yourself on a *Joy Date*. Choose to share this joy date with someone other than your child. This date is about reconnecting with your own joy when it's not wrapped up in the joy your child is or is not experiencing.

Supplies

- ❏ This book
- ❏ Pen
- ❏ Whatever needed to enjoy your joy date

Directions

1. Begin with prayer. Ask God to help you practice being joyful with the blessings He has in your life without being tied to the happiness of your child.
2. Consider things and places that bring you joy. Don't overthink this. For example, one thing I love to do is sit in my backyard with my camera and wait for the hummingbirds to appear so I can take their picture.
3. Make a plan for your day. Write it down. Here. In this book. Writing it down will help make sure you go through with it.
4. Go on the joy date.

5. Come back here and journal about it. Write down what you liked most about it. Add a line or two about where you'd like to go and what you'd like to do for your *next* joy date.

THE GOD OF OUR CHILD'S DECISIONS

For the LORD gives wisdom; from his mouth come knowledge and understanding. (Proverbs 2:6 NIV)

One of the scariest aspects of my child leaving the nest is trusting their decision-making skills. This is when I begin second-guessing how well I did as a parent. The doubts mounted when I asked myself if I'd really done everything I could to equip them for this time in life.

This was not a path any parent should take. Because truthfully, the answer is no. I did *not* do everything I could have or should have. The fact that my shortcomings as a parent could open my child to danger or pain is terrifying to me.

But in those moments of regret, I have had to remember that I'm not the one who has the ultimate responsibility for equipping my child. That is God's responsibility. He often has used me to impart knowledge and wisdom to my kids, but God is bigger than any and all my mistakes—omission or commission.

When each of my children left home, this was probably my biggest worry—what would happen when they made a mistake and I wasn't there. God's ability to keep them safe no matter what was brought home to me one day after two of my three sons had left home.

These two experienced outdoorsmen took their boats out for a daytrip on the river. I knew they were going and I was concerned because it was late summer so pop up thunderstorms were normal. I worried about them getting caught in one of those storms while on the water. But they weren't worried, so with my, "be careful" ringing in their ears, off they went.

I didn't hear from them that evening. I wanted to call and see how they were, but was afraid I'd be labeled a worrying mother, so I waited until morning and asked our youngest son how it went. He grinned at me and would only say I needed to call one of the other two and let them tell me. With my heart pounding, I grabbed my phone and called.

Sure enough, a thunderstorm had come up in the distance. But before they could paddle to shore, something happened. To this day, they don't really remember the incident. The time between paddling toward shore and when my oldest son came to was approximately two hours. He wasn't on the shore in his boat, but in the river, caught on a snag in the river by his life vest. It took him several minutes to locate his brother who was just regaining consciousness on the edge of the river several yards away.

From the burns where they were touching the water, they knew they'd been struck by lightning—or at least the water around them had been struck. They both had headaches and lethargy for a couple of days, but came out of that experience wiser and no worse for wear.

Just like God has often worked through my mistakes, I can trust Him to do the same for my children. I know that when my child makes a decision that leads them astray, God is with them, even when I'm not.

A PRAYER
for My Child's Decisions

But as for you, continue in what you have learned and have firmly believed, knowing from whom you learned it (2 Timothy 3:14 ESV)

Dear Lord, I agonize over the possibility of where my child's decisions can lead. My experience has given me greater perspective. Sometimes that's a good thing and sometimes it's not. I wish I didn't see some things so clearly.

I struggle with when to step in and share my knowledge, as opposed to when to keep my mouth shut. I don't want to interfere with the plans you have, but I also don't want to stand by when I can keep my child from possible pain.

You have a plan for my children. I know that plan will include any poor decisions they may make. Why can't I rest in that instead of fretting over a future outcome that hasn't even happened yet? You are the only One who knows exactly where each decision will take my child. I can trust You, I know that. I've seen You work in my life and in the life of my child.

Show me how to be still and wait for You to work. In those times when Your plan is for me to speak, give me the spiritual ears to hear Your Spirit clearly. Continue to protect my child from poor choices and from the poor choices of others. Amen.

CREATIVE CONNECTION
Spiraling from Worry to God

Sometimes our worries can spiral out of control, leading us places we don't want to go. Today we'll let our worries lead to the firm foundation of God's Word.

Supplies

- ❏ Bible
- ❏ This book
- ❏ Pen
- ❏ Things to decorate the page (colored pencils, stickers, washi tape, etc.)

Directions

1. Start with prayer. Are you noticing a trend here? I try to begin everything with prayer and the practice has stood me in good stead.
2. Next, write the word GOD in the middle of the blank space provided.

3. Now, draw a spiral out from the word. Make sure you have room to write in between the lines of the spiral.
4. Where the spiral ends, write a word that sums up something you're worried about your child deciding.
5. Find a Bible verse that answers your concern, or puts your worry to rest. Write that Bible verse in between the lines of the spiral.
6. Decorate the page as you wish.

SCRIPTURE PRESCRIPTIONS

- *For we are God's handiwork, created in Christ Jesus to do good works, which God prepared in advance for us to do. (Ephesians 2:10 NIV)*

- *The LORD says, "I will guide you along the best pathway for your life. I will advise you and watch over you. (Psalm 32:8 NLT)*

- *Now faith is the assurance of things hoped for, the conviction of things not seen. (Hebrews 11:1 ESV)*

chapter three
RELEASING SADNESS

As I've mentioned before, I'm not a fan of change. In fact, I'm downright resistant for it—even when I know it's a good thing. I've been known to answer a suggestion with an emphatic *no*, before I've even heard the full idea. I'm not proud of this knee-jerk reaction, but I am aware of it. That awareness is what has allowed me to begin to make some changes.

Just like I can get attached to certain ideas, sometimes I can get attached to certain emotions. These feelings can be good or bad, doesn't matter. But occasionally I wear them so long that I don't want to change them. Sadness is one that can quickly become a habit for me. I have to be on guard against cozying up to this emotion.

The empty nest season was difficult for me because I got into the habit of feeling sad—especially when our first son left home for military service. I let this melancholy color everything I did. Before I got a handle on it, it had begun to affect our entire family.

Just like bad behavior, difficult emotions are contagious and they can lead us places we don't want to visit.

The only way I combat this tendency is by practicing ways and reasons to release sadness.

When we choose to leave sadness behind, God does amazing things. Of course God is always at work doing amazing things, but sometimes we miss them if we're focused on sadness.

God has shown me that even through the most difficult circumstances, there are reasons to be thankful. Then, that gratitude so often leads to joy. When a child leaves home—no matter the reasons—we can find ways to share their excitement. It's up to us to tap into those reasons to be joyful and work from there.

WHEN NOT HOVERING IS HARD TO DO

The eyes of the LORD are everywhere, keeping watch on the wicked and the good. (Proverbs 15:3 NIV)

I fight a two-fold curse as a parent—I worry and I hover. I think those habits stem from the fact that I'm a control freak about every aspect of my life. This control tendency is something I've had to fight constantly, at times more successfully than others.

I also love to be involved in my kids' lives. I adore just being around them. This fuels my inclination to hover. I've discovered that the hardest time for me to *not* hover is when they leave home. I just can't seem to help myself.

God tends to illustrate principles to me through nature. When I searched my mind for examples when hovering is bad in nature though, I came up empty. Birds hover and this action helps them make sure there are no predators around. Fish hover for the same reason. Even my beautiful hummingbirds have good reasons for hovering.

Had I missed something? Was hovering really a *good* thing? I was on my back porch when I continued to ponder this idea and that's when the truth of why hovering is a bad habit came to me. I realized that all these animals hover because they are responsible for their own safety or the safety of their families.

That was the part of the puzzle I was missing—I'm *not* the one responsible. God is. By hovering, I'm trying to take on the responsibility that is God's. God is excellent at doing His job. Where I'm a failure because I can't be everywhere and see everything, He can. We can trust Him with our kids and leave the hovering to Him.

A PRAYER
When We Want to Hover

Fathers, do not exasperate your children, so they won't become discouraged. (Colossians 3:21 HCSB)

Dear Lord, I'm struggling with this new dynamic between me and my son. He's been safe at home all his life and now he lives somewhere else. I want so badly to call and text him hourly. So far I've resisted the impulse, but resisting is harder and harder.

I know my child and when I get carried away with hovering, he retreats. I don't want to push him away by checking in with him too often.

The problem is the fact that I know so many of the things that can go wrong when someone is first living away from home. I want to keep him safe from those pitfalls and unwise decisions. I also know that it's through some of my own bad decisions that I've earned the most valuable lessons.

Help me walk the line between being overprotective and being there when he needs me. Only You know the best path through this transition time. Give me ears to hear Your whispered direction and then strengthen my faith to follow. Your path brings peace, mine is paved with the sharp rocks of fear. Hold my hand, even as I held his when he was baby, and lead me safely into Your peace. Amen.

CREATIVE CONNECTION
Learning to Not Over-Manage

Letting go isn't one of my natural strengths, although I should be good at it by now since it seems to be something God asks me to do frequently. Sometimes this tendency shows up in unexpected places—like baking scones. I enjoy cooking, but I'm far from an expert at it.

But one thing I've learned to do well, bake scones. But it took me a while to master this skill. The reason? I had in mind how the dough should look and that led to over kneading. Scones that are worked too much are tough. So I've learned to stop before I think it's time and let the dough have room to develop like it's supposed to.

So today our creative connection is baking scones. I'm including a basic recipe, but feel free to add something like blueberries, chocolate chips or raisins to it. Just remember to *not* over knead the dough.

Supplies

- ❏ Kitchen with an oven and basic tools for cooking
- ❏ 2 cup all purpose flour
- ❏ 1 tablespoon baking powder
- ❏ 4 tablespoons sugar
- ❏ ½ teaspoon salt
- ❏ 6 tablespoons butter
- ❏ 1/2 cup milk (you can substitute heavy whipping cream for richer scones)
- ❏ 1 large egg

Directions

1. Preheat oven to 425° F and line a baking sheet with parchment paper.
2. Sift together flour, baking powder, salt, and sugar. Add the butter using a pastry cutter or your fingers. Mix it until you have crumbs the size of small peas.
3. In a separate bowl mix together milk and egg until fully combined. Do not overmix.
4. Add wet ingredients to the dry ones and stir until just combined. The mixture will be crumbly at this point.
5. Turn the dough out onto a floured surface and knead until the dough holds together into a ball. Flatten into a circle and cut the dough like a pizza into 8 equal triangles.
6. Transfer to the baking sheet, leaving about half an inch between each scone and its neighbor.
7. Bake at 425° F for 16–20 minutes or until the tops are lightly browned and the dough is cooked through.
8. Remove to wire rack and cool completely.

AM I FOCUSED ON THE RIGHT THINGS?

Love bears all things, believes all things, hopes all things, endures all things. (1 Corinthians 13:7 ESV)

I love celebrating my kids' accomplishments. When they were just toddlers, I received some excellent advice from a friend to make an effort to look for things my kids were doing right, instead of what they were doing wrong. I did a pretty good job at this—when they were young.

Then they grew and life got crazy, I'd slip into the habit of focusing on the negative instead of the positive. One day one of my sons brought this to my attention. It had been a hard week at middle school—for all of us. He had lost his homework, forgotten to study for a test, had a disaster zone for a room and, the last straw, made all of us late for school. I dropped his brothers off, parked, and moved him to the front seat. Then I proceeded to unload all my frustration at his behavior on him. When I finally wound down, he looked up at me with tears in his eyes. "Am I ever going to get life right?"

I felt like the worst mother ever. As bad as I felt, I could see he felt even worse. I apologized and tried to reassure him before I let him go into the building. That afternoon I arranged for someone else to pick up the other two boys from school so I could surprise this son with an impromptu mother-son time.

I've never forgotten the way my focus on all the things he did wrong had hurt my son, I realized I'd begun making the same mistake when my kids left home. I found myself focusing so much on what was or could be going wrong, that all I did was worry and fret. When it finally dawned on me what I was doing, I made an immediate effort to shift my focus.

The result of that decision had a waterfall result I didn't expect. First, I found a lot more peace. Then I noticed that my conversations with my kids became much more positive and easier. When I'd been concentrating on the negative, I'd have to guard my tongue to keep from commenting on all the things I saw that might have been wrong. Now, comments and connections were natural and the words just flowed. By pointing out what they were doing right, they seemed to feel more free to bring up things they were struggling with.

A PRAYER
to Reset My Focus

Above all, keep loving one another earnestly, since love covers a multitude of sins. (1 Peter 4:8 ESV)

Dear Lord, I've fallen back into a bad habit. I don't mean to, but it seems like all my focus is on the things my son is doing wrong as he gets ready to move out. I know this isn't the time to criticize and nag, but I can't help it. Lord, change my focus. Make it so I see all the things he's doing right.

I know the reason I'm doing this is because I'm panicking. I feel like my time to correct and give advice is running out. My response is driven by fear, not by faith. Help me trust the lessons You've provided while he was growing up. You have prepared him for what comes next and I must let go and trust You. But it's so hard.

I've always been my child's safety net—ready to catch him before he falls into disaster—or at least nearby to help when life does come apart. I don't want that to change. But I know my role is changing, no matter how hard I fight it.

You are always with him and You—not me—have always been his safety net. You've allowed me to be part of that, but I know when I'm not there, You already have someone else who'll be used by You to keep my son on the right track. Amen

CREATIVE CONNECTION
Finding the Right Focus

One of the first things I learned when I got my camera was how to focus. As easy as that sounds, it's a skill I'm still working on perfecting—forty years later. My dad was a professional photographer and if he were still alive today, he'd be amazed at the powerful cameras we have—in our cell phones. These tiny devices far surpass most of the equipment he used for his award-winning images.

Today's creative exercise is going to involve your cell phone camera. Your participation doesn't rest on what type or brand of phone you have. *Any* cell phone, with a camera, will work. After we're done, you'll journal about what God showed you through this exercise.

Supplies

- ❏ This book
- ❏ Pen
- ❏ Cell phone

Directions

1. Begin with prayer and ask God to give you insight into your current situation.
2. Go outside and find several small items to focus on. You can choose a flower, blade of grass, pebble, really anything will work. The goal is to photograph something we don't usually focus

on. We want to get close and see all the details. This is a specific kind of photography called macro photography.
3. Hold your cell phone camera as close to the object as you can. Now slowly pull your phone away until the item is in focus. Repeat this process with at least three things.
4. Answer the following questions:
   a. Did you notice it was hard to keep the phone steady when you're so close?
   b. Did you notice you must have space between the camera and the object or else the photo will be super blurry? This space between the subject and the camera is referred to as *length of focus*.
   c. Did you notice each item, in each specific setting needed a slightly different length of focus?
   d. How can you apply these answers about focus to your situation with your child?
5. Journal all your answers in space provided and write what God shows you. Finish with a prayer of thanksgiving.

RUNNING TOWARD LETTING GO

I shall run the way of Your commandments, For You will enlarge my heart. (Psalm 119:32 NASB)

Many of my memories are tied up with my child's independence. I remember when he began to sit up, walk, and talk. The first time I left him at preschool kept me in mixed emotions all day. I was thrilled because he was growing up and devastated at the same time. The years followed with nights away with friends, summer camp, middle school, and driving. Each of those milestones left a mark on my heart. Each one strengthened my faith—and my prayer life.

With each milestone, I found myself telling myself, *just breathe, God's got this.*

What I didn't know was that I was in training for one of the hardest pinnacles in parenting—the empty nest. Thankfully God didn't ask me to let go of my child all at once. In His faithful wisdom, He provided ample ways to practice.

While I never embraced running as a hobby, I've known many who did—and several who regularly run marathons. Before I knew better, I'd always assumed that the way a person practiced for running a marathon was to first work your way up to running twenty-six-and-two-tenths miles and keep running that distance regularly.

Nope. That's not the way it works at all. Turns out a runner trains regularly for a year or more working up to weekly mileage goals. These relatively shorter runs build stamina without requiring the regular marathon distances. These regular runs are sometimes ten-plus miles long, interspersed with days of practicing sprints—which together build stamina and increase lung function as well as muscle strength. Increasing oxygen intake is critical to running a race of this length. Marathon runners have stronger—and larger—heart muscles, able to pump more oxygenated blood and provide what these athletes need to sustain them.

God does the same kind of training schedule with us as parents. He gives us times when parenting life feels like a sprint, other situations call for us to stay the course as we build up endurance. But through it all, He's instilling in us the breath of the Holy Spirit to give us the capacity to run the parenting race without collapsing.

A PRAYER
for the Parenting Marathon

Therefore, since we are surrounded by such a huge crowd of witnesses to the life of faith, let us strip off every weight that slows us down, especially the sin that so easily trips us up. And let us run with endurance the race God has set before us. (Hebrews 12:1 NLT)

Dear Lord, being a parent is getting harder, not easier. When my kids were babies, sleep deprivation and colic were horrible events. Then came the terrible twos and their battle for independence. I won that battle for a while, and I really thought the hardest parts of parenting were past.

I might have won a skirmish or two, but the battle for independence has been won by them. That is the way it should be. You created us to stay for a while under our parents' watchful eyes before moving into adulthood. When that was my journey to independence, the process seemed right. Now, as a parent, it seems like such a bad idea.

Please forgive me. This final sprint toward independence has left me exhausted. The more tired I get, the more my emotions take over. Restore my strength so I can finish this race well. I don't want my child's remaining time at home to be a battle ground. Instead, show me how to join them in the race for independence.

You didn't design me to be my child's adversary. I know You want me to be his biggest cheerleader, urging him to finish the race well and step over the finish line into independence. Give me all I need to be all my child needs right now. Amen.

CREATIVE CONNECTION
Training for a Prayer Marathon

Don't panic, I'm not suggesting something dangerous or even strenuous. Just a little stretching of our prayer muscles—in case we ever need to run a prayer marathon.

Prayer is a two-way street, like any healthy conversation. Today, we'll begin a program to build our endurance for listening to God, as well as talking to Him. This will be done over the course of one month—twenty-eight days works equally well if you're not using the calendar. You can begin anytime and count out twenty-eight days or you can wait until the beginning of a month.

The critical point of this exercise is to avoid being legalistic about the practice of prayer *while* staying consistent. Don't label yourself a failure if you miss a day here and there.

Supplies

- ❏ Bible
- ❏ This book
- ❏ Journal with at least thirty blank pages
- ❏ Pen

Directions

1. Prayerfully consider your days and your schedule. Are you an early riser or a night owl? Do you work outside the home? Are you a caregiver or do you volunteer somewhere regularly? Take all of this into account before setting your goal.

2. Set an end goal. For example, at the end of twenty-eight days I want to be able to spend forty-five minutes a day in prayer without watching the clock or getting unreasonably distracted. You can use that goal, but you don't have to. Pray about it and choose a goal.
3. Decide when you'd like to plan your prayer time. Sometimes life happens and there will be days when you may have your prayer practice at a different time and that's fine.
4. In the space provided, write out WEEK ONE and below that, number 1 – 7. Do the same for weeks two, three, and four.
5. Beside week one, write the goal you want to have mastered at the end of that week. Do the same for weeks two, three, and four.
6. When you begin the process, I recommend reading a short passage of scripture and praying. Work on spending as much time *listening* as you do speaking. Toward the end of your prayer time, write a couple of thoughts in your prayer journal that occur to you.
7. On the days you stick to your routine, make a note. You can put the scripture reference of what you read or the time or just a check mark. The important thing is to honestly record your progress.
8. As the days progress, notice changes. Is it easier to spend time in prayer? Do you miss the time with God if something interferes? Write down all your insights either here or in your prayer journal.

WHEN THE EMPTY NEST LOOKS DIFFERENT

Do not be anxious about anything, but in every situation, by prayer and petition, with thanksgiving, present your requests to God. (Philippians 4:6 NIV)

My husband and I are both fairly well-educated adults. Because of our personal life experiences, we always expected our sons would follow our examples, moving from high school to college and on into life. God had different paths in store for our children though. And as a parent I found myself initially unwilling to embrace the options our kids chose. My unwillingness came close to destroying precious relationships.

Our oldest son was the first one to choose differently. He left high school and went directly into the Marine Corps, where he served two combat tours in the Middle East. I had always expected to have college as a sort of trial run before the ultimate empty nest, but no, that wasn't part of God's plan.

When he first went away, I focused completely on the negatives—the empty space at the dinner table, the inability to hear his voice, the holidays that just felt wrong. Coloring every moment of each day was my own fear of what he was and would be facing. I struggled against anger—I was mad at our son, at my husband for not figuring out a way to stop this, and ultimately I was mad at God.

In the midst of this emotional hurricane, I came to a place where I knew I had to have God's help to make it through. I needed His strength and comfort. I needed to again renew my faith in the absolute truth that God was taking care of my son.

Kids fly the nest for a lot of reasons and in a lot of ways. The only common denominator between each instance is the certainty that God loves them even more than we do. Beyond that, we must remember He's the *only* one who can always be with them. I had to discard a ton of expectations wrapped around the idea of an empty nest, but the one thing I didn't have to leave behind was God. He was there when I was angry, when I was terrified, and when I turned back to Him. Knowing this has allowed me to let go of my other children with a little bit more confidence and peace.

A PRAYER
for Difficult Days of Letting Go

In peace I will both lie down and sleep; for you alone, O LORD, make me dwell in safety. (Psalm 4:8 ESV)

Dear Lord, this isn't what the empty nest transition is supposed to look like. I always anticipated my child's path to independence with joy. That journey was to have been a slow change from fully dependent, to partially dependent, to adulthood. The transition shouldn't have been so sudden.

Please forgive my fear and frustration. I know that none of this caught You by surprise. You know the beginning from the end and everything in between. I have somehow forgotten to look to You instead of getting so caught up in my expectations.

I feel like my child isn't ready for the steps he's taking. It breaks my heart that I can't make that decision. You are in control. I'm rehearsing all the faithfulness You've shown throughout my child's life. I will cling to that as life hits hard.

Reassure me, through other people, Your word and the peace that passes all understanding. I need that peace right now—desperately. I want to be strong for my child but this quick pivot has brought me to my knees. I have to smile, to my knees is exactly where I need to be to weather the change of season.

Wrap Your loving arms around my child and keep him safe. Don't let him go through this transition feeling alone. Lift him up and put people around him to act as Your guard while he gets comfortable with this new situation. You are the One we can all trust. Amen.

CREATIVE CONNECTION
A Library of Comfort & Reminders

Learning to accept letting go can sometimes be a process, especially if the event that made you let go happened suddenly. To help me in those seasons, I've built a tiny, portable library of reminders and encouragement. You'll do that through this creative exercise. I have several envelopes in my office, each one is for a specific difficulty I've faced, from writer's block to illness to grief. I can grab the envelope, pull out the contents and find myself smiling and feeling refreshed in mere minutes. That's your goal with this project.

Supplies

- ❏ Bible
- ❏ This book
- ❏ Envelope
- ❏ Magazines or anything that has pictures you can cut out
- ❏ Glue stick
- ❏ Index cards
- ❏ Things to decorate the index cards (colored pencils, stickers, washi tape, etc.)

Directions

1. Begin with prayer. Ask God to equip you for the difficulties you're facing now and the difficult days in your future.

2. Cut your index cards to fit into the envelope you chose.
3. Spend some time copying Bible verses on the index cards, one per card.
4. Look through the magazines and pull out pictures that speak to you. Choose the pictures without worrying about doing this wrong. Some may choose peaceful landscapes, others may gravitate to cartoon characters or superheroes. Affix each picture to an index card with the glue stick.
5. Decorate the index cards as you wish or not at all.

VALUE IN THE NEW NORMAL

*Consider the ravens, that they neither sow
nor reap; they have no storeroom nor barn,
and yet God feeds them; how much more valuable
you are than the birds! (Luke 12:24 NASB)*

The season of emptying the nest can throw us off. What was once normal seems anything but. Things we took for granted are suddenly cause for celebration.

As our kids grow life can sometimes get crazy. While their needs for parenting aren't as constant, the need are just as urgent. Getting ready for a child to fly the nest brings a flurry of activity. Because of this, the quiet after they're gone can seem even more intense and leave us feeling unnecessary. But there are things we can do to continue to play an active role in our new fledglings' lives.

In the wild, many young birds leave the nest before they're proficient at flying. Some tumble out accidently and some leave because that's the way God designed them. Some species even learn to fly *after* they've left the nest. But these young birds aren't abandoned by their parents. These bird parents will stick close to fledglings on the ground, protecting them from predators and even bringing them food.

When our kids fly the nest, we can also still be an active part of their lives. That activity won't look the same as before, but our presence is just as important. In this season, we are the ones who must make the effort to stay connected. While our kids are exercising their wings, they will often avoid—or even forget the value of—asking for help.

No matter what, we can rest in the fact that just as God has a plan for the birds, we can rest assured He has a plan for our families as well.

A PRAYER
to Embrace Life's New Normal

Be strong and courageous; don't be terrified or afraid of them. For it is the LORD your God who goes with you; He will not leave you or forsake you." (Deuteronomy 31:6 HCSB)

Dear Lord, help me as I adjust to this new normal. Life is so strange without my child safe at home. Reassure me that where he is, he is safe. I'm so used to being the one my child turns to when he needs something. Now I'm no longer right there. He'll have to learn to rely on himself and on those You bring to help him.

Give my child insight as he learns to fly solo. Don't let him forget I'm only a phone call away. Protect him from poor decisions, unsavory companions, and the schemes of the enemy. Show him how to exercise the wisdom You've given him already.

Protect him from the pitfall of pride. Don't let him be too proud to ask for help when he needs it. Give him insight to judge those he goes to for counsel. Keep him far from anyone who would influence or entice him away from You.

Don't let him fall for the snares of the enemy. Show a spotlight on the situations that lead to disaster. Help him to always turn to You first. I know you're his first and best line of defense when life comes at him with overwhelming in mind. Amen.

CREATIVE CONNECTION
Watching the Birds

Sometimes we learn by doing, sometimes we learn by watching. Most often we learn through a combination. Today we'll focus on letting go by watching the birds.

I've discovered that when I'm struggling, it helps me to physically get outside and look up. This gives me a physical reminder to think beyond myself and look up in a spiritual sense. In addition, birds are always fascinating to watch and I learn so much that I can apply spiritually.

Supplies

- ❏ This book
- ❏ Pen

Optional Supplies

- ❏ Binoculars
- ❏ Camera

Directions

1. Begin with prayer. Ask God to show you something that helps open your eyes about your current situation,
2. Go outside. Another option is to visit a local zoo or someplace that has a bird habitat.
3. Get comfortable and scan the sky for birds. Begin by observing them in flight.

4. Listen. How many different bird voices can you distinguish?
5. Now answer the following questions:
   f. How do different birds fly?
   g. How many birds do you see?
   h. Does the same type of bird always fly the same way?
9. While you observe, jot down your thoughts in the space provided. Write about the spiritual application to what you observe.
10. Finish with a prayer of thanksgiving.

SCRIPTURE PRESCRIPTIONS

➣ *A thief comes only to steal and to kill and to destroy. I have come so that they may have life and have it in abundance. (John 10:10 HCSB)*

➣ *He heals the brokenhearted And binds up their wounds. (Psalm 147:3 NASB)*

➣ *For God is not a God of disorder but of peace—as in all the congregations of the Lord's people. (1 Corinthians 14:33 NIV)*

chapter four
FINDING JOY IN THE CHANGES

I love the phrase, *finding joy*. Yes, there are many times when joy bursts on us unaware. But in times of stress and challenge, I often have to go looking for joy. Sometimes it's as hard to find as a four-leaf clover, and at other times joy is obvious with my first glance. The good thing is this, the more I search for happiness, the more I find of it. God's joy, just like God Himself, is always there, ready to be found when we look.

Sometimes when we're in difficult situations, we must rely on other tools to help us find those things to rejoice in. One of the best tools I've found is gratitude. For me, I find it impossible to be sad when I look at all the blessings God has put in my life. Joy is also contagious. I love being around happy people because they infect me with their way of looking at life.

Other times in my life I've had to sneak up on joy because it was elusive and hard to hold onto. During those times, journaling is a tool that helps me capture and not lose the reasons to be joyful. Writing things down helps do two things. First, the act of writing cements the joy in my mind and heart. Second, I can refer back to those written words and recapture joy that has drifted away.

Change is hard, you'll get no argument from me about that. But just like a bird who has to go through a molting period to get new feathers and fly stronger and faster, change is so often a catalyst to new blessings God has planned.

NEW JOY

Rejoice in our confident hope. Be patient in trouble, and keep on praying. (Romans 12:12 NLT)

When I think of new joy, I think of things being added to my life. The addition of a new baby, a new home, or even a new pet. I rarely think of new joy in terms of losing something. But through the empty nest season, I've learned that perspective is the biggest part of the joy battle.

When a child leaves home, we can often slip into a period of mourning. While I think it's fine to acknowledge the difficult feelings that come with new seasons, we don't want to hang out there for very long. The now empty—or emptier—nest can also carry a lot of new joy in these changed circumstances.

I'll never forget the joy and pride on our son's face when he looked into his future in a new place. His smile matched the one he had when he first learned to walk.

That is exactly what our kids are doing when they leave the nest. They are learning to walk all by themselves.

This doesn't mean we won't be close enough to help if they need us. But just like we can't spend their lives carrying them physically, we also can't carry them once they reach this stage of life.

What we can do is celebrate with them. When our kids leave the nest, it truly is a time of celebration—for them and for us. We have completed one phase of parenting. Now is the time to praise God for working through us—through our mistakes and through the things we got right. This is also a time to celebrate our kids. They are embarking on a wonderful—slightly scary—life-long adventure. By spending time rejoicing with them and reminding them of all they've done well, we set them up for success and joy in the future.

A PRAYER
to See the New Joy

Then he said to them, "Go your way. Eat the fat and drink sweet wine and send portions to anyone who has nothing ready, for this day is holy to our Lord. And do not be grieved, for the joy of the LORD is your strength." (Nehemiah 8:10 ESV)

Dear Lord, this is such a joyful time for my child, and such a sad time for me. I'm going to miss her so much. I know I should be celebrating her leaving home, but I'm struggling. My mind won't stop thinking about all I'm losing.

Help me replace the sadness with joy. Show me how to use her excitement to jumpstart mine. I know I'm being selfish. I really do want the best for my daughter. I'm just overwhelmed with memories.

The time I've had with her in my house has gone by so fast. Just yesterday she was learning to walk and today she's walking out the door. I feel like she's leaving not just our home, but me. I know that's a lie. She'll always be my child, nothing will change that. But that relationship already looks different.

Help me to be okay with different.

Show me the joy in the change. Replace my sadness with a sense of accomplishment. Not that I've done so great. You know how many ways I've failed. But You, Lord, You have been amazing. I'm so proud of the woman my daughter has become. And that's where I'll start. I'll begin with gratitude and trust that the joy and peace will follow. Amen.

CREATIVE CONNECTION
Practicing Gratitude

Gratitude is foundational to experiencing joy. Finding ways to be thankful can be even more important when we're in a new season and may not recognize our blessings. To help combat this, we'll need to begin a one-month gratitude journal.

I have kept a gratitude journal almost continually for the past twenty-plus years. I began because I recognized the fact that I'm not a naturally grateful person. I needed some help. I can honestly say that keeping a gratitude journal changed my life.

Supplies

- This book
- Blank journal
- Pen
- Bible

Optional Supplies

- Things to decorate your journal (colored pencils, stickers, washi tape, etc.)

Directions

1. As always, before you make each entry, pray. Ask God to show you the blessings in your life that you can be thankful for.

2. Each day, list three things you're thankful for. You can add a line or two about why you're grateful, but you don't have to.
3. Do not repeat anything you list for the entire thirty days.
4. Each day, find a Bible verse that speaks to you about gratitude. Either write out the verse each day (preferable) or just record the scripture reference.
5. At the end of your thirty days, in the space provided, come back here and journal what you learned.

SUPER BLOOM

And God is able to make all grace overflow to you, so that, always having all sufficiency in everything, you may have an abundance for every good deed; (2 Corinthians 9:8 NASB)

I don't know about others, but for me as a parent, my kids' teenage years were a challenge. Some weeks it felt like one storm after another. This kind of upheaval was only natural. God was awakening the drive to leave home in our kids and they frequently tested the limits of their independence.

However, in the midst of the conflict, I had trouble keeping my perspective. My emotions went from the extreme of wanting them gone *now*, to wanting to hold them even tighter. That season was trying for everyone.

When I was little, my parents used to take frequent trips out west. My dad was a college professor and a photographer so he had the time and the impetus to see the world. I remember one spring trip when we arrived in Death Valley after an unexpectedly wet winter. While rain in that region isn't unheard of, it is unusual. That kind of season only comes about every ten years or so.

Because of the unusual weather that winter, we were treated to the most amazing super bloom of wildflowers—in the desert. My photographer dad was in heaven. What made the trip all the more memorable was the fact that this wasn't our first time to visit Death Valley. I knew—from experience—how dry and desolate that part of the country is.

That's what the empty nest feels like to me. A super bloom of joy coming after a long winter of rain. All the seeds we planted throughout their lives are bursting into bloom.

A PRAYER
While We Wait for a Super Bloom

Let us not become weary in doing good, for at the proper time we will reap a harvest if we do not give up. (Galatians 6:9 NIV)

Dear Lord, what a stormy season we're facing as a family. One day life is chaos and struggles, the next day is full of incredible anticipation. Throughout the parenting years we've had ups and downs—sometimes too extreme. But never so many compacted into such a short time.

I know You're about to do something amazing, but we're having a bumpy ride on the way to that. Give us all a supernatural dose of grace toward one another. Help us hang on tight to You and choose joy no matter what obstacles appear.

Our tempers are frayed and emotions are overwhelming us all. Spread Your inexplicable peace into every corner of our home and our lives. We need a big dose of that peace to get through this empty nest preparation season.

Give us a taste of the super bloom to come. I almost see the edges of that season of abundant blessings for my child, but I don't think he can see past the struggles he's facing as he tries to get there. Show me how to help him cease striving and rest—especially when every fiber of his being has him straining toward his new life. Use me as his ally, not his enemy. Keep us both from choosing adversarial roles. Show us how to choose Your love and see one another through Your eyes. Amen.

CREATIVE CONNECTION
Insight from a Rose

Flowers are a beautiful gift from God. But within their structure, we can find spiritual insight. Today we'll glean some wisdom from a rose.

Supplies

- ❏ This book
- ❏ Bible
- ❏ Pen

Optional Supplies

- ❏ Things to decorate your journal (colored pencils, stickers, washi tape, etc.)

Directions

1. Begin with prayer, asking God to provide insight and the ability to recognize what He has to share with you.
2. In the space provided, draw three rectangles, leaving room below for notes. Label each:
   a. Rose
   b. Thorn
   c. Bud
3. In the *rose* box, write something that has been a positive in this time of empty nest.

4. In the *thorn* box, write something that has been a challenge in this time of empty nest.
5. In the *bud* box, write about something new that has come from this challenging time.
6. Journal your thoughts about what God is showing you. Repeat this exercise on the days when you need some help finding joy.

LETTING PERFECT JUST HAPPEN

The LORD will guide you continually, giving you water when you are dry and restoring your strength. You will be like a well-watered garden, like an ever-flowing spring. (Isaiah 58:11 NLT)

One day I was out taking pictures of the spring tulips. I was doing great with the close-ups and with choosing just a single flower to highlight. But trying to get a pleasing arrangement from the groups was much harder than you might think. There's always one that's either past its peak or not in the right place.

I confess to being a perfectionist. I like things in my life to be just so. If they're not, sometimes I can get a tad bent out of shape. That makes parenting a challenge. I have in my mind a picture of how I want life to go. However, we all know things rarely turn out as planned.

But on this photography day, I got lucky. I walked up and the tulips were in perfect order and at their peak of their blooms—all five were pastel perfection. They looked like a master flower arranger had come by and put them in order. I didn't have to do anything except notice them and snap a picture.

The thought occurred to me that I needed to remember that lesson in regard to my kids. I'm bad about trying to over-arrange things, especially with my kids. I have a tendency to *tinker* with circumstances so everything will go just right.

Instead, I need to stop and look around. God has ordered the lives of my kids perfectly. He really does *not* need my help. He knows the best time and circumstance for each of my kids to leave the nest. I don't need to fret and worry. I need to have faith in the Master Arranger and just be ready to applaud when He unfolds the perfect plan.

A PRAYER
When Things Aren't Perfect

Surely there is not a righteous man on earth who does good and never sins. (Ecclesiastes 7:20 ESV)

Dear Lord, our life is far from perfect right now. As our family struggles to embrace this coming season of an empty nest, we need Your perspective. I confess to trying to over manage each day. I'm trying to make enough last-minute memories to sustain me through the lonely days ahead. I can see that my actions are adding stress to an already challenging season, but I can't seem to stop.

Show me what it looks like to rest in You during this time. I want everything to be perfect. Even more than that, I want my son perfectly prepared. But I'm not in charge of perfect, am I? You are the only One who can orchestrate circumstances and bring order and provision from times of chaos and uncertainty.

Help me release my frantic hold on life. Flood my anxious soul with Your peace. Use me to bring tranquility instead of trouble into these days. Keep me from being the source of unrest. Allow me to give my child the gift of a joy-filled transition. Only You can orchestrate this in me and I fully surrender to Your sustaining love and grace. Amen.

CREATIVE CONNECTION
All Lined Up

I think one of the main reasons I avoided expressing creativity through drawing and doodling was because what I did wasn't ever good enough. I absolutely hate missing the mark. More than that, I hate making a mistake that can't be fixed.

This was also the reason I'd purchase beautiful blank journals and then never use them. I just didn't want to mess them up with a mistake. When I faced this tendency head on, I decided to take steps to fix it. So, I began doing two types of things. First, I do things that left room for mistakes. Second, I refused to let myself throw something out because of a mistake. Instead, I forced myself to find a way to turn a mistake into something beautiful.

This creative exercise is one that will leave room for mistakes while practicing order and mindfulness.

Supplies

- ❏ This book
- ❏ Black, fine-tip pen
- ❏ Ruler

Directions

1. Begin with prayer, asking God to show you something He wants you to know about yourself, your child, or the situation.

2. In the space provided, draw a box. Take up most of the space on the page, and use your ruler. It doesn't have to be perfect, but it helps if the lines are straight.
3. Use the space to draw random lines in all different directions. Make sure the lines go from one side of the box to the other, but don't continue outside the box. Vary the angles, some up and down, some from corner to corner, some from side to side. Vary the space between the lines. Your lines should cross over each other.
4. Stop and look at the random chaos. It may be interesting, but it's not a masterpiece. Yet. Sometimes life can look like this—a bunch of random lines. They're stark and don't make a lot of sense and they're not really all that pretty to look at.
5. At each intersection, where the lines meet, use your black pen to color in tiny triangles. So, each two intersecting lines will now have an anchor.
6. While you color, spend time in conversation with God. Ask Him how He's using this situation to bring new joy and how you can help anchor each random intersecting point in your life and your child's life with joy.

Here's a tiny example to help you visualize what you're working toward:

REJOICING IS *NOT* SELFISH

Why am I so depressed? Why this turmoil within me? Put your hope in God, for I will still praise Him, my Savior and my God. (Psalm 43:5 HCSB)

Have you ever experienced parental peer pressure? I certainly have. If you're not certain what I'm talking about, let me explain. Parental peer pressure is like any other type of peer pressure and something most of us have experienced. Sometimes this pressure is inadvertent while other times it can be deliberate.

I felt it particularly on my oldest son's first day of school. I remember meeting friends for coffee after we'd dropped off our kids. I walked into the restaurant and was met with a table full of crying mothers. I instantly felt out of place and out of step.

While I did feel a pang when I dropped my son at school that morning, his excitement about school had been infectious. Truthfully, I was glad to have a couple of hours all to myself.

But confronted with the grief I saw in my peer group I immediately felt like a horrible mother. I thought there might have been something wrong with me because I wasn't in full-blown mourning about the morning. So, I faked my way through a quick cup of coffee and left as soon as I could.

I went home and pulled out my Bible and my journal. I hadn't been able to pour out my feelings in that setting, but God was a safe place to process the turmoil in my soul. I came across the verse above and felt peace flood my soul.

God relieved my guilt and helped bring order to the turmoil I felt. Occasionally we experience seasons when we want to weep and jump for joy at the same time. God's gifts are multi-layered and unexpected. I can't wait to unwrap the next season He has in store for me, no matter what.

A PRAYER
for Relieving My Guilt

Search me, God, and know my heart; test me and know my anxious thoughts. (Psalm 139:23 NIV)

Dear Lord, I feel so out of step with other parents during this season of a newly empty nest. I am sad my daughter has taken this step, but I'm also so excited about what You have for me. I've loved being a parent, but at times, that role has eclipsed so many things I've wanted to do.

Now I feel like a new world is open before me and instead of rejoicing, I find myself with doubts and guilt. I know this season is part of Your purpose for my life and for my daughter. Shouldn't I rejoice in it then? Why am I so torn? Lord help me to discern if I've done something wrong.

Replace my uncertainty and sense of guilt with Your peace. Help me not to look at how others in similar situations are coping and judge my path by theirs. Give me eyes to see You as the only judge of where I am and how I'm doing. Amen.

CREATIVE CONNECTION
Recognizing False Guilt

None of us is perfect. While we each need to take care to confess the things we do wrong, it's not good to embrace false guilt. God doesn't expect us to live condemned. His plan is for us to live in freedom. This creative exercise will help us expose some of the lies and false guilt we've embrace and banish that condemnation from our lives.

Supplies

- ❏ Bible
- ❏ This book
- ❏ Pen

Optional Supplies

- ❏ Things to decorate your journal (colored pencils, stickers, washi tape, etc.)

Directions

1. Begin with prayer. Ask God to help you recognize the false guilt that is burdening you right now.
2. Write 1 John 3:20 across the top of the space provided.
3. List the things you are feeling guilty about. You don't have to be specific, just a word or two so you know what each item refers to.

4. As you write things down, ask God if that is something you've really done wrong either by commission or omission. If the answer is yes, ask God's forgiveness. If the answer is no, scratch it out.
5. When you're done with your list, use part of the space to journal about the experience and what God has taught you about yourself and about Him.
6. End with a time of prayer, thanking God for His wisdom and love.

WHITE SPACE

I pray that your hearts will be flooded with light so that you can understand the confident hope he has given to those he called—his holy people who are his rich and glorious inheritance. (Ephesians 1:18 NLT)

I grew up in a creative family. My mother is an internationally known watercolorist and mixed media artist. My dad's first career was as a classically trained musician. He played in the symphony and was a music professor at several prominent universities. His second career, after he had a major heart attack, was as a landscape photographer.

The principals of design, color, and lighting were practically encoded in my DNA. From an artistic viewpoint, I've always known the value of negative space, which is a place in artwork or design where the eye can rest. I explored my own creativity—choosing words as my medium. I discovered this concept of negative space has another name—white space. For publishing, white spaces refers to the amount of space on a page that is *not* filled with text. As our lives have become busier, and the cost of paper and printing is no longer a driving force for economy, the publishing trend is to always include plenty of white space.

I love to apply these interchangeable concepts to us as empty nesters. Life can feel very empty after a child leaves home. The change of circumstances can feel like negative space because it's really not fun. But God has helped me change the way I looked at this season of life. Instead of viewing it as negative, He has invited me to view it as white space.

The time—the place where my eyes can rest—is a gift from God. While it is different, it's also a time to reconnect with God and refocus on the plans He has for my life. By doing this we're not abandoning our children or minimizing their importance in our lives, we're setting a healthy example. I'm using this white space as time to set my eyes on God and let Him renew my soul.

A PRAYER
to Accept the Gift of White Space

Thank God for this gift too wonderful for words! (2 Corinthians 9:15 NLT)

Dear Lord, this is a different season for me. My daily duties as a parent are gone. When my child flew the nest, so did my familiar to-do list. Life hasn't changed in every way. I still have work to accomplish every day and places to be. But there are chunks of activity missing.

This open space makes me uncertain. I know the time will eventually fill up with a familiar routine, but right now it's not familiar. Help me see this season and the open schedule as a gift instead of a loss. I want to use this as a pause to focus on You and what You want me to do going forward.

Change is hard for me and I know I often reject *different* just because I'm unfamiliar with the newness. Let me recognize this tendency before I let my reactions reject what You have for me. Every season in my life, even the difficult ones, have held joy. At times I have an easier time finding the joy, but You always provide it. Make sure I remember the lessons of Your past faithfulness to sustain me where I find myself now. Amen.

CREATIVE CONNECTION
Beautiful Scribbles

Times of transition can often feel chaotic, but within the chaos can be unexpected white space. The key is learning to find these unexpected gifts. This creative connection is designed to help us find beauty in the white spaces of our lives.

Supplies

- ❏ Bible
- ❏ This book
- ❏ Pen
- ❏ Colored pencils or markers

Directions

1. Begin with prayer. Ask God to reveal what you should do with the new white space in your life right now.
2. Using circular motions, make a scribble in the space provided. Don't fill up the space completely, keep your scribble loose and leave some white space.
3. Use some of the larger white spaces to write Bible verse references to verses about rest and peace.
4. Use some of the medium white spaces to write positive single words, such as rest, peace, joy, etc.
5. Finally, fill some of the smaller areas with color.

6. When you finish look at the unexpected picture you've created out of the random scribble.
7. Pray a short prayer of gratitude for the unexpected white spaces God has provided in your life right now.

SCRIPTURE PRESCRIPTIONS

→ *The LORD your God is with you, the Mighty Warrior who saves. He will take great delight in you; in his love he will no longer rebuke you, but will rejoice over you with singing." (Zephaniah 3:17 NIV)*

→ *Always be Joyful (1 Thessalonians 5:16 NLT)*

→ *But let all who take refuge in you rejoice; let them ever sing for joy, and spread your protection over them, that those who love your name may exult in you. (Psalm 5:11 ESV)*

chapter five
FOCUSING ON NEW MEMORIES

After endings, beginnings.

God has rhythm for our lives, an ebb and flow much like the tides of the ocean. Sometimes we don't understand all the forces at work, but we do know the One who has dominion over all of creation. Even when seasons of chaos make life appear out of control, God is at work.

The empty season is one of those times that often bring chaos. The tide of emotions rises and floods our lives with so many feelings all at once, we feel overwhelmed. We need to give ourselves time—time to process and realign with the new normal. Once we can do that, we are ready to focus on the new memories that are forming. God has given us the opportunity to enter a new season in our parent/child relationship.

I would always be a parent, and my son would always be my son, but he wouldn't always be a child. With the empty nest, he was well on his way to becoming the man God had always planned for him to be. I didn't ever want to get in the way of God's will. In some ways, I wanted my son to stay young. In other ways, I was so ready for the transition to be finished so I could breathe a sign of relief.

We're years past the empty nest and that sigh of relief hasn't happened yet. I still worry, just about different things. I no longer tell him what to do, but when asked, I do offer advice. And I pray. I can easily say I have prayed more intensely since my son left home than I ever did when he lived under my roof. My prayer life hasn't intensified because I'm better about being disciplined in prayer. I think the intensity has come because I'm no longer intimately involved in the day-to-day workings of my son's life. Whatever the reason. My prayers give me ample opportunity to remain a vital part of his new life.

What a wonderful ride this new season has been. I've loved all the new memories and opportunities to interact with him on an adult level now. God is faithful. When He removes something, He fills the spot with something else. I've seen again how all of God's gifts work together to bring us closer to Him.

SUNSET, SUNRISE

Then God said, "Let there be lights in the expanse of the heavens to separate the day from the night, and they shall serve as signs and for seasons, and for days and years; (Genesis 1:14 NASB)

Being a photographer, I have two favorite times of the day—sunrise and sunset. I love every type of light these two events produce. Sometimes the light is intense in the depth of the color and the variety. Other days produce perfect pastels that only last a moment before they disappear.

If you nail me down and force me to choose one absolute favorite, I would pick the sunrise. There's just something about the stillness of new beginnings that speaks to my soul. But I don't always get to choose. Sometimes circumstances and physical location determine which event I take part in.

That's the way life is with empty nests. We begin the journey to an empty nest the day our kids are born. Sometimes the empty nest is delayed, but no matter whether it comes slower or faster than we expect, it does come for almost all parents.

Just like a sunset, that time of life is beautiful. Having a child leave home is a major milestone in parenting. This is a time when we need to accept the fact that God has accomplished something great—and used us in the process. We need to appreciate the beauty of it, even if it carries the undertone of ending.

Just like the sun sets in nature, it also rises the next day. Parents face their own sunsets. But we need to hold tight to the truth that sunset is just a precursor to a beautiful sunrise—the next step in parenting and that step will bring beauty in ways we have yet to experience.

A PRAYER
for Sunsets

From the rising of the sun to the place where it sets, the name of the LORD is to be praised. (Psalm 113:3 NIV)

Dear Lord, I feel like I'm at a sunset time of life with my child leaving home. It's an intense time, and there is beauty here. But I'm having trouble seeing past the darkness that appears to loom on the horizon.

I don't want to feel only sadness at this new season in my son's life. I want to be able to experience all the joy that's happening around me and the joy that's to come. I feel so silly because tears seem to clog my throat at the most inappropriate times. What is wrong with me?

I want to say so much to my son. I want more time for long conversations about his life, but time is moving too swiftly. Just like the sun races toward the horizon, this chapter of our lives is racing to the end.

Remind me of the sunrise to come. You are doing a new thing in my son's life and in all our lives. Your plan is good—meant for blessings and joy. Along this new path we'll find opportunities to connect in new ways. Help me look forward to the new things. I don't want to forget, but I also don't want to cling so hard to the memories that I miss what's happening now.

Open my hands so You can fill them with blessings. Keep my mind fixed on You as I savor every moment You're giving me now. Amen.

CREATIVE CONNECTION
Witness the Light

Sunsets are beautiful, but when the sun sets on a season it can carry sadness. After the sunset—unless you live near one of the poles—darkness dominates the landscape. In the physical world this allows our bodies the rest they need so they can begin fresh again the next day.

I believe the same can be said for seasons. When events come in quick succession it can be overwhelming. We need that peaceful darkness for a time to give us a place to rest and process.

This creative exercise is designed to help us process the progression and rhythm of life.

Supplies

- ❏ This book
- ❏ Pen

Optional Supplies

- ❏ Camera (can be a cell phone)

Directions

1. Begin with prayer, asking God to guide you and give you the insight you need for this time of life.
2. Look at your calendar and check the weather. Choose two clear or only lightly cloudy, consecutive days. You will need to find a place

where you can watch the sunset and the sunrise the next morning. It should be the same place. Don't watch the sunset from one location and the sunrise from another. You don't have to see the horizon, although that's fun if it's feasible. You can choose your backyard. The only important thing is that you can see the sky.

3. On the evening of the sunset, go outside about twenty to thirty minutes before the actual sunset. If you want, take some pictures. Notice the light and the sounds you hear.
4. When the sun is fully down, use the space provided to jot down your thoughts about the sunset and how your empty nest resembles a sunset.
5. The next morning, get to the same place about twenty to thirty minutes before the actual sunrise. If you want, take pictures. Notice the light and the sounds you hear.
6. When the sun is fully up, use the space provided on the next page to jot down your thoughts about the sunrise and how your empty nest is also a time of new beginnings.

ENCOURAGEMENT WHEN THE CLIMB HAS BEEN HARD

Holding fast to the word of life, so that in the day of Christ I may be proud that I did not run in vain or labor in vain. (Philippians 2:16 ESV)

Parenting can feel like an uphill climb. My husband and I live in the foothills of the Blue Ridge Mountains. When we can, we love to hike those hills. But we're not getting any younger and our joints aren't what they used to be. We've found we need incentives to stay the course for those uphill sections. Usually we keep climbing because we know the view will be worth it.

Recently we decided to tackle a new hike because of the beautiful waterfall at the end. We'd put off the experience because the trip to the waterfall was all uphill. But the pictures I'd seen of the beautiful setting convinced me to give it a go.

About an hour-and-a-half into the hike, we questioned our decision. Even with frequent breaks and plenty of water, we were reaching the end of our endurance. While I sat on a convenient rock, trying to catch my breath, a couple, even older than us, came down the trail. The woman smiled at me. "I sat on that same rock on the way up. Don't give up, you're only steps away and the view is more than worth the effort you've put in."

I thanked her and hauled myself to my feet. Sure enough, not even fifty steps farther the ground leveled out into a gorgeous scene and magnificent waterfall. She'd been right. The climb was worth every bit of effort I put into it, although it did take me a few minutes to catch my breath and relax enough to enjoy all that I could see.

Parenting is like that. So often raising kids feels like an uphill climb—one that's well beyond our abilities. The process of parenting is beyond our abilities, but the climb is not beyond God's.

Reaching the time for emptying the nest requires special endurance and encouragement. Each of us finds that encouragement different ways. Some of us focus on the end result and how beautiful it will be when our child is living with joy and fulfillment as an independent adult. For others, it helps to look back, remembering the times when our child's steps toward independence brought joy.

We must find the strength to look forward. If we're not careful, we will find ourselves arriving winded and unable to appreciate the beauty of what's before us. When that happens, we need to take time to catch our breath and look around. God has provided beautiful moments, even in the letting go. Watching our kids strike out on their own and become more of who God planned them to be is beautiful. And He's given us encouragers who walk the path before us. God truly is able for every challenge we face.

A PRAYER
When You're Out of Breath

For I will satisfy the weary soul, and every languishing soul I will replenish." (Jeremiah 31:25 ESV)

Dear Lord, I'm looking for a way to catch my breath. The process of getting my child ready to leave home, coupled with the actual leaving has left me exhausted. I'm tired mentally, physically, and even spiritually. I've poured myself into this process and while there have been tearful times, I feel a sense of well-being.

But in the emptiness of exhaustion, I'm developing doubts. Fear is creeping in and I'm too weak to hold it at bay. My mind conjures up what-ifs faster than I can bat them away. I need You, Lord. I crave the sweet peace that can only come from You.

Fill me with the strength of Your Spirit. Renew my equilibrium and give me something solid to cling to while I breathe. This has been a joyful time. The unexpected blessings are too numerous to count. But they've come so quickly, I can't keep up. I don't want to miss a single one. Give me time to process all that's happened in our family. Amen

CREATIVE CONNECTION
Freedom Doodling

One thing I love to do to relax is doodling. I love to see where my mind goes when I just let go. One thing that inspires me in this practice is something I refer to as freedom doodling. I made up the name, but it fits how I feel. I will introduce you to this creative exercise to help you slow down and relax when you feel like life is pushing you and you barely have time to take a deep breath.

Supplies

- ❏ Praise music (can be hymns, classical, or modern praise and worship)
- ❏ This book or a journal with empty pages
- ❏ Pen, pencil, colored pencils, or markers—something to doodle with

Optional Supplies

- ❏ Things to decorate this page (colored pencils, stickers, washi tape, etc.)

Directions

1. Begin with prayer. Ask God to give you breathing space and renew your strength.
2. Turn on praise music.

3. Settle yourself in a comfortable place where you can doodle. I prefer a table, but many can doodle with a book in their laps.
4. When the music begins, put your pen to the paper. Listen to the beat of the music and let that guide your movements. Make dots or lines or circles. Just let your mind be blank and your hand guide your pen or pencil.
5. When another song begins, change colors and repeat the process.
6. Your goal with this creative connection isn't a finished piece of art, it's a calm soul. Just have fun.
7. When you're finished, breathe a prayer to God thanking Him for this time in your life.

THE GIFT OF SILENT STILLNESS

*It is good to wait quietly for deliverance from
the LORD. (Lamentations 3:26 HCSB)*

I like to stay busy. I have a lot of trouble sitting without doing something. And I love white noise—music, audio devices, and television in the background is a big part of my daily life. But I'm learning to embrace times of silent stillness as well.

Parenting brings with it lots of activity and lots of noise. The absence of noise when children are in the house is a definite warning that something might be going wrong.

Years of seeing the silence in a negative life has left a mark. Accepting the gift of silence takes effort. Being silent and still carries the same awkwardness I used to feel when speaking in front of a group. I just don't know what to do with my hands or the rest of me. Nothing about it feels natural.

Experiencing an empty nest feels like that too. Now the silence *really* carries a negative feeling—one of longing. I remember in those first few days doing my best to stay busy, but I'd still find myself walking through now clean and almost empty rooms. This gift wasn't one I was ready to accept.

But I decided to try.

Instead of pacing the house, I began spending more time with God—through prayer and reading His word. And slowly, almost without even noticing the change, I saw the gift of silent stillness for what it was.

Quiet wasn't something to be feared or feel guilty about. The silence became one of the joys of this new season. Instead of increasing the perceived gap between me and my child, the silence gave me opportunities to pray and remember the many blessings. This, in turn, increased my joyful anticipation of what would come next for my kids and for me. God never leaves a void without giving us the opportunity to fill it with Him.

A PRAYER
for the Stillness

And he awoke and rebuked the wind and said to the sea, "Peace! Be still!" And the wind ceased, and there was a great calm. (Mark 4:39 ESV)

Dear Lord, I freely confess that being still isn't my favorite thing to do. I love being busy and about my work. Stillness feels uncomfortable and wrong. Stillness is where I find myself in this transition. The work of helping my child move on is done and I'm at a loss as to what comes next.

I walk from room to room, satisfied with a job well done, sad at the unusual neatness, and unable to be still. When I pause, my feelings overwhelm me. The whirlwind of my thoughts scares me. There are things I don't want to think, but I know they are there. If I'm still, they'll come to the surface and I'll have to deal with them.

That's the real issue with stillness—having to confront things I'd rather leave untouched. Hold my hand as I submit to the stillness. Remind me there's nothing to dread. Show me that my fears are ungrounded. My child is safe in Your hands. The stillness isn't a dark closet to dread, it's a quiet oasis of time spent with You. Amen.

CREATIVE CONNECTION
Morning Words

Sometimes the easiest and hardest time to be still is in the morning. Mornings can be rushed. lazy, and everything in between. Mornings can also be a wonderful time to practice mindful stillness. I want to challenge you to begin your morning differently for the next seven days.

Supplies

- ❏ This book
- ❏ Pen

Optional Supplies

- ❏ Things to decorate this page (colored pencils, stickers, washi tape, etc.)

Directions

1. Prepare the space on the next page by writing each day of the week for seven days, beginning tomorrow.
2. Every morning, before you're even fully awake or out of bed, grab this book and a pen. In the space that corresponds to the day of the week, write the first thing that comes to mind.
3. NOTE: The first time I tried this, the first day my entry was: "Why did I agree to this crazy exercise?

I'm not awake this early." If this happens to you, write it down and go on.
4. Repeat this routine for seven consecutive days.
5. At the end of the seven days, journal about what you discovered by being mindful first thing in the morning.

EXPERIENCING TRUE JOY IN MY CHILD'S INDEPENDENCE

Dear brothers and sisters, when troubles of any kind come your way, consider it an opportunity for great joy. (James 1:2 NLT)

Some kids are more independent than others. Our sons seemed to race toward independence from the moment they were born. "I can do it myself" was the war cry more often than not. Although I wanted them to learn to cope without my immediate attention, every step away from needing me brought a little pain. A lot of parenting is like ripping an adhesive bandage off one hair at a time.

Don't get me wrong, I did find joy in many milestones—especially getting finished with potty training. But at other times, their independence brought more anxiety than joy—like learning to drive. And I would have to dig deep to find the joy. I discovered early on there is a difference between finding joy and choosing to experience it.

I'm a little independent too. When things happened that I wasn't ready for, my attitude wasn't the best. I didn't like the stress that came with our kids driving alone, so I refused to find the joy in it. That short-sighted decision kept me from experiencing a lot of joy while our kids were growing up. But over time I learned my lesson and when it came time for each one to fly the nest, I was ready to look for the joy in the middle of the upheaval, and fully experience those happy times.

I'm so glad I did.

Even in the midst of my tears, I could feel the joy. There was the excitement of each child as he walked into the next phase of life. There was also the anticipation of having more time with others I care for—my husband, my other kids, friends, and even extended family members. Raising kids takes up a lot of space in our lives and when one leaves the nest, we are given the gift of more breathing space.

God has provided joy in every step of parenting, if we'll only look for it. Sometimes we have to search for it. Other times the joy is obvious. But the most important thing is to accept it and experience it to the fullest.

A PRAYER
As I Experience Joy

Give thanks to the LORD, for he is good; his love endures forever. (1 Chronicles 16:34 NIV)

Dear Lord, there is joy in this season. You've shown me that while my child has left home, there is so much to be excited about in this new part of our journey. I want to praise You for what You've done in both our lives. I've had the privilege of watching my daughter grow into a strong young woman. This is Your hand at work and I thank You for all You've done.

You've allowed me glimpses, through the years, of who You had planned for her to become. Now I see the total picture. Thank you for allowing me to be part of the process—especially since there were so many times I was more of a hindrance than a help.

Through this journey You have been faithful. You've used the good times and the difficult ones to bring my child to this wonderful place. In the process, You've grown and stretched me in ways I wouldn't have thought possible. I'm so grateful for Your patience with me when I resisted what You were showing me.

Help me to remain grateful in the process of letting go. I confess there are times when I want to stop or slow down. But Your plan is perfect, even in the timing. Amen.

CREATIVE CONNECTION
Prayer Walk

I love prayer walks of all types. I love walking around or through a space that I know will hold God's people while I pray for God to work. I love to walk through neighborhoods and sections of a city, asking God to break down walls and begin to make His presence known in a way that cannot be ignored. Mainly, I just love to walk and talk to God.

This last creative connection will introduce you to this opportunity. I encourage you to talk a long walk and talk to God specifically about your child. Ask Him how specifically to pray and where He wants you to join Him as He works in your child's life. While you're walking and talking, don't forget to spend plenty of time listening.

Supplies

❏ Walking shoes and a place to walk
❏ This book
❏ Pen

Optional Supplies

❏ If you're close by, you can plan your walk in the vicinity of where your child now lives. Walk the streets and paths you child walks and pray while walking.
❏ Pull out a map (or print one) that shows where your child is now staying. Use your finger instead of your

feet and do a virtual prayer walk around the area of your child's home.

Directions

1. Take a walk.
2. While you're on the walk, use the time to talk to God about your child.
3. When you get home, use the space provided to record your thoughts and insight.

PUSHING *THEM* INTO JOY

All your children shall be taught by the Lord, and great shall be the peace of your children. (Isaiah 54:13 ESV)

Not every child is happy about growing up. Some of our kids look at leaving home with anxiety and dread. When that happens we're sometimes put into the position of encouraging them to the very thing we dread.

We have a much-loved goof of a dog. Cosmo is an eighty-pound couch potato. He enjoys cuddling next to us and sometimes will even crawl into our laps. He's a mutt, but is blessed with a beautiful thick, black coat of hair. We live in the south and summers are not his favorite time of the year. His fur is much more suited to a cooler climate. He's obedient, though and he's always good about quick trips outside for personal reasons.

When we moved, our new home had a beautiful, fenced yard and we expected Cosmo to love it. He does love it—now. But he didn't start off that way. The first time we opened the back door he took one look at the new-to-him expanse of grass and tried to turn back to the house. We coaxed, petted, and resorted to bribery with his favorite treat. Nothing would make him budge on his own. Finally, we snapped on the leash, pulled him into the yard, and shut the door so he couldn't get back in. He looked at us like we'd beat him.

We ignored his sulks and sat in nearby chairs to give him time to get accustomed to the new setting. Sure enough, up came the nose as he caught the scent of something interesting. That whiff led to a tentative step and another and another. Pretty soon he was exploring—but keeping a watchful eye on us to make sure we weren't abandoning him. My husband got up, played with him, and after a few false starts Cosmos was racing around his new yard, happy as he'd been in our previous place.

Introducing and enticing a reluctant child into leaving home can be a lot like getting our dog accustomed to the backyard. We need to remain supportive and visible—without giving in to anxiety. Even when every fiber of our parenting heart wants to keep our kids safe at home, we have to help them embrace the path God has and rest in the certainty that He is always with them. In the process, our certainty can become their joy and that's a gift worth giving our kids.

A PRAYER
for Helping Our Kids Move On

Now may the God of hope fill you with all joy and peace in believing, so that you will abound in hope by the power of the Holy Spirit. (Romans 15:13 NASB)

Dear Lord, help me to be an example of courage and joy for my child. I know he's reluctant to leave the nest. I also know that he is ready. You have equipped him to take the next step in becoming the man You have planned for him to be.

I know part of his fear has been fed by mine through the years. I haven't been a fan of change and I'm afraid this has influenced him. Take away his fears and replace them with confidence in You and in Your plan.

This time is hard for me. Even though You've shown me it's time, sometimes fears of what might happen overwhelm me. Don't let this tendency add to his struggle. I don't want to make things harder for my child.

Help me conquer my own trepidations and, in turn, help him to conquer his. Don't let my child look to me as the best example. Turn his eyes to You and help him stay focused on You. You have his best always in Your plan. Remind him of that.

When the fears make him stop, hold his hand and remind him Your love conquers all—even those things we're wary of facing. Give him a glimpse of the joy to come when he steps out in faith and follows Your path. Guide and direct him as You have all his life. Use this time to draw him closer to You as he learns to lean on You. Amen.

CREATIVE CONNECTION
The Power of a Letter

Letters are powerful ways to show we care, even more now because it's so rare to send or receive one. This creative exercise is to write a letter to your child. No cheating allowed, write the letter in long hand, no typing, no email, no text, and no card with a preprinted message.

Supplies

- ❏ Paper
- ❏ Envelope
- ❏ Stamp
- ❏ Pen
- ❏ This book

Directions

1. Pray before you begin to write the letter. Ask God to give you the words He wants you to write and for the discipline to follow through on finishing and mailing the letter.
2. Write the letter. I'm not going to give you any more direction on the content of the letter. I trust the Holy Spirit to lead you in the direction He knows is best.
3. Address the envelope. And don't forget the stamp.
4. Mail it.
5. In the space provided, journal your thoughts about writing the letter. Now, consider who else God may want you to write a letter to.

SCRIPTURE PRESCRIPTIONS

●◆   *The steadfast love of the Lord never ceases; his mercies never come to an end; they are new every morning; great is your faithfulness. (Lamentations 3:22-23 ESV)*

●◆   *Then the One seated on the throne said, "Look! I am making everything new." He also said, "Write, because these words are faithful and true." (Revelation 21:5 HCSB)*

●◆   *This is the day that the LORD has made; let us rejoice and be glad in it. (Psalm 118:24 ESV)*

ACKNOWLEDGMENTS

A book never comes to light without a community behind it. I want to try to recognize all the precious people who stand with me and behind me while I write each book.

Foremost is my God and Savior. He's the One who called me to write with Him. It's a joy I hope will never grow dim.

Not far behind is my amazing husband, Kirk Melson. He gives me the daily—sometimes hourly—encouragement I need to stay the course. His love, partnership, sense of humor, and willingness to do anything around the house is a gift beyond price.

I also want to thank the fantastic team at Bold Vision Books. including Karen and George Porter, Rhonda Rhea, Larry J. Leech II, Maddie Reyna, and Amber Weigand-Buckley. These are my people. They get the vision and bring it to light so much better than I could ever imagine.

My agent extraordinaire, Blythe Daniel, is someone who deserves my heartfelt thanks for her insight and unfailing support—even when I disappear because of life's unexpected difficulties.

A writer's journey is so much sweeter because of the special companions God provides to walk along with us. In that I want to thank my sister-friend, DiAnn Mills, as well as my newest constant traveling companion, Edwina Perkins.

I wouldn't be the writer I am without my writing buddies: Lynette Eason, Tammy Karasek, Alycia Morales, Molly Jo Realy, Lynn Blackburn, Linda Gilden, Emme Gannon, Michelle Cox, Tim Suddeth, and Michelle Bengtson. These fellow scribes are voices of reason, as well as a cheering section when I put pen to paper.

Finally, but by no means last, are those who provide the constant prayer support I so desperately need. Thank you to my daily prayer partner, and fellow author, Beth Vogt, and to my dear friend, Linda Goldfarb. Also, I want to recognize the amazing women in my Friday morning accountability group: Valorie Moore, Sherri Jones, Tara Allen, Tarah Smith, Sally Given, Juditha Chapman, Vicki Suddeth, Christie Anderson, Liz Petruzzi, Dodie Denton, and Martie Bailey, I couldn't do this without you.

MEET EDIE MELSON

EDIE MELSON has walked through the empty nest season several times and in several ways—from sending a son off to war at age eighteen, to sending another off on a round-the-world mountain climbing trek. With each situation she has been quick to share how God is faithful in all ways and at all times.

Edie uses the truths God has taught her as a mother, wife, photographer, and author to encourage others. She's learned to embrace the ultimate contradiction of being an organized creative. As an author, blogger, and speaker, Edie has empowered and challenged audiences across the country and around the world.

Her books reflect her passion to help others call on God's strength during challenging times, often using creativity to establish and strengthen this connection. She also knows the necessity of Soul Care and leads retreats, conferences, and workshops around the world on ways to use creativity to help strengthen our connection with God.

She and husband Kirk have been married forty-two-plus years with three grown sons and three grandchildren. They live in the foothills of the Blue Ridge Mountains and can often be found with their big black dog hiking the mountains.

Connect with her at **www.EdieMelson.com** and through social media.

www.ingramcontent.com/pod-product-compliance
Lightning Source LLC
Chambersburg PA
CBHW070154100426
42743CB00013B/2909